REWARDS® *Writing*

Sentence Refinement

Student Book

Anita L. Archer, Ph.D.
Mary M. Gleason, Ph.D.
Stephen L. Isaacson, Ph.D.

Assisted by

Pat Pielaet
Scott Ricker
Johnathan King

Sopris West™
EDUCATIONAL SERVICES

A Cambium Learning Company

BOSTON, MA · LONGMONT, CO

Published and Distributed by

Sopris West™
EDUCATIONAL SERVICES

A Cambium Learning Company

4093 Specialty Place ■ Longmont, Colorado 80504

(303) 651-2829 ■ www.sopriswest.com

Contents

Contents

Letter to students from the REWARDS Writing authors

Dear Students,

Welcome to the REWARDS Writing program. This program will teach you how to improve your writing by (a) making better word choices and (b) writing more advanced sentences. For example, you will learn how to go from a sentence such as:

We went to the big department store.

to a more interesting sentence such as:

After we got off the subway, we raced to the huge department store to find the latest rap album.

In every lesson, you will work on making better word choices by selecting more precise words and by moving away from overused words. In the example sentence, the author replaced "went" with a more interesting word, "raced." Similarly, instead of using the overused word "big," the author selected the word "huge."

Every day you will also be learning how to polish your sentences by combining ideas and expanding your sentences. You might answer questions such as when, where, why, and how within a sentence to convey more complete and interesting ideas to the reader. In the example sentence, the author told us <u>when</u> they went to the store (*after we got off the subway*) and <u>why</u> they went to the store (*to find the latest rap album*). As a result of this "sentence polishing," the author wrote a much more interesting and informative sentence.

Finally, you are going to practice a strategy for editing your paragraphs so that the sentences sound good and the words represent your best word choices.

We know that this program will improve your writing. While it will be fun, it will also take THINKING.

Anita Archer
Mary Gleason
Steve Isaacson

PART A *Sharpening Your Word Choices*

Although the jacket my mom gave me was ~~nice~~, it was too

small. When I returned the jacket to the shop, the store clerk

gladly exchanged it. She was very ~~nice~~. I found shopping there

to be a ~~nice~~ experience.

CAUTION AHEAD

DETOUR

p. 209

PART B *Polishing Your Sentences (Sentence Combining)*

1. Start: Josh has a train set with 80 feet of tracks.

   Add: The train set is electric.

   Create: ***Josh has an electric train set with 80 feet of tracks.***

2. Start: The tracks cover the garage floor.

   Add: The tracks are winding.

   Create: _____

   _____

   _____

1

3. Start: Buildings line the tracks.

Add: The buildings are tiny.

Create: _____

_____

4. Start: Josh pretends that the train delivers things to the buildings.

Add: The buildings are miniature.

Create: _____

_____

_____

PART A   *Sharpening Your Word Choices*

On his trip to Italy, Marcus visited a ~~big~~ castle built in

the 1300s. As he strolled up to the castle, ~~big~~ statues of former

rulers greeted him. Inside, he was awed by the ~~big~~ rooms.

Outside, the castle was surrounded by ~~big~~ gardens.

PART B   *Polishing Your Sentences (Sentence Combining)*

1.   Start: Many people in Union City are immigrants.

      Add: The immigrants are from Cuba.

      Create: ***Many people in Union City are Cuban immigrants.***

2.   Start: Life in Union City is an adjustment for them.

      Add: The adjustment is huge.

      Create: _____

_____

_____

3. Start: They had to leave many belongings behind.

Add: Their belongings are precious.

Create: _____

_____

_____

4. Start: However, they feel very welcome in their country.

Add: Their country is new.

Create: _____

_____

_____

PART A — Sharpening Your Word Choices

The country was in very ~~bad~~ condition. The schools,

hospitals, and community services had become very ~~bad~~

because of the country's ~~bad~~ leaders. Finally, a few brave people

stood up to their ~~bad~~ leaders and demanded a new government.

PART B — Polishing Your Sentences (Sentence Combining)

1. Start: A meadow is an environment.

Add: The environment is lively.

Create: _____

_____

2. Start: Butterflies flit from flower to flower.

Add: The butterflies are colorful.

Create: _____

_____

_____

3. Start: White-footed mice scurry through the grasses.

Add: The grasses are tall.

Create: _____

_____

_____

4. Start: A hawk swoops down and grabs one of the mice.

Add: The hawk is red-tailed.

Create: _____

_____

_____

PART A   *Sharpening Your Word Choices*

For a number of reasons, people say that Alicia is pretty.

First, she is very healthy and, as a result, has ~~pretty~~ skin

and hair. Second, she always wears ~~pretty~~ clothes that match

her personality. But, best of all, she has a ~~pretty~~ smile.

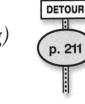

PART B   *Polishing Your Sentences (Sentence Combining)*

p. 211

1. Start: The Dane is a popular dog.

     Add: The Dane is noble.

     Add: The Dane is great.

     Create: ***The noble Great Dane is a*** _____

popular dog. _____

2. Start: It has a head.

     Add: The head is long.

     Add: The head is rectangular.

     Create: _____

_____

3. Start: The Great Dane has front legs and thighs.

    Add: The front legs are straight.

    Add: The thighs are powerful.

    Add: The thighs are muscular.

    Create: _____

_____

_____

4. Start: Its coat gives the Great Dane a glossy appearance.

    Add: Its coat is short.

    Add: Its coat is thick.

    Create: _____

_____

_____

PART A *Sharpening Your Word Choices*

On a chilly Saturday night, campers gathered around a ~~hot~~

campfire. The campers warmed their hands on mugs of hot,

steaming cocoa. Flames leaped high above the ~~hot~~ logs.

~~Hot~~ sparks shot into the air and lit the night sky.

PART B) *Editing Your Paragraph*

Sound good?
Combine?
Omit?
Replace?
Expand?

a. As you read the paragraph aloud, ask yourself, "Does it **sound good**?"

b. **Combine** sentences 1, 2, and 3.

c. **Combine** sentences 4, 5, and 6.

d. **Combine** sentences 7 and 8.

e. **Combine** sentences 9 and 10.

¹In the 1700s, the Tigua Indians found nourishment in the desert. ²The nourishment was ample. ³The desert was arid. ⁴Cactuses provided a food source. ⁵This food source was plentiful. ⁶The food source was nutritious. ⁷In addition, the Tiguas used land near the Rio Grande river to grow corn, squash, and beans. ⁸The land was rich. ⁹The Tiguas also ate animals, such as rabbit, deer, and snake. ¹⁰The animals were available.

Edited paragraph:

_____

_____

_____

_____

_____

_____

_____

_____

_____

_____

_____

_____

6

PART A *Sharpening Your Word Choices*

Three ~~little~~ children walked to the lake. They were amazed to

see thousands of ~~little~~ brown toads on the shore. The children

had never seen toads so ~~little~~. The ~~littlest~~ child ran all around,

grabbing at the toads. She tried and tried but never caught one.

PART B *Polishing Your Sentences (Sentence Combining)*

1. Start: Matthew saw many farm animals at the fair.

Add: The fair was annual.

Add: The fair was in the county.

Create: _____

_____

_____

2. Start: His favorites were the sheep.

Add: The sheep were white.

Add: The sheep were curly-haired.

Create: _____

_____

_____

3. Start: He also liked seeing the rabbits.

Add: The rabbits were tiny.

Add: The rabbits were spotted.

Create: _____

_____

_____

(**PART A**) *Sharpening Your Word Choices*

Several smart middle-school students were studying together.

Each person thought that the others were ~~smarter~~. Brian was

a very ~~smart~~ guy. He amazed everybody with his card tricks.

Sharon was a ~~smart~~ girl. She could do math problems in her

head faster than anybody. Lucy was probably the ~~smartest~~

of the group. She was so ~~smart~~ that she could probably skip high

school and go to college.

(**PART B**) *Polishing Your Sentences (Sentence Combining)*

1. Start: The music in elevators calms people.

   Add: The music is bland.

   Add: The elevators are public.

   Add: The people are frazzled.

   Create: _____

   _____

   _____

2. Start: However, other people would rather listen to music.

Add: The music could be loud.

Add: The music could be energetic.

Create: _____

_____

_____

3. Start: One person suggested music.

Add: The person was witty.

Add: The music was live.

Create: _____

_____

4. Start: Would you like sharing an elevator with a rock band?

Add: The elevator is small.

Add: The rock band is live.

Create: _____

_____

_____

8

(**PART A**) *Sharpening Your Word Choices*

The Arctic Islands region of Canada is quite beautiful and very cold. When you fly over this region, you see hundreds of ice-covered islands. When you land on one of the islands, you are immediately confronted by ~~cold~~ weather and ~~cold~~ winds. You find little relief from the ~~cold~~ temperatures.

(**PART B**) *Polishing Your Sentences (Sentence Combining)*

1. Start: Cubs have fur.

Add: The cubs are newborn.

Add: The cubs are polar bears.

Add: The fur is very little.

Create: _____

_____

_____

2. Start: To protect the cubs from Arctic temperatures, the polar bear digs a den in the snow.

Add: The Arctic temperatures are frigid.

Add: The polar bear is the mother.

Create: _____

_____

_____

_____

3. Start: Inside the den, the mother keeps the cubs near her body.

Add: The cubs are defenseless.

Add: Her body is warm.

Create: _____

_____

_____

4. Start: As the cubs grow fur, they spend periods of time outside the den.

Add: The fur is thicker.

Add: The periods of time are short.

Add: The den is warm.

Add: The den is protective.

Create: _____

_____

_____

_____

PART A *Sharpening Your Word Choices*

Galileo was the first to look at the moon through

a telescope. He wrote about what he saw and helped other

people understand how ~~good~~ a telescope could be. Galileo was

a ~~good~~ scientist. He analyzed his observations carefully and

kept ~~good~~ records of his procedures and results.

PART B *Polishing Your Sentences (Sentence Combining)*

1. Start: Percy Julian discovered many uses for the
soybean plant.

Add: The uses were wonderful.

Create: _____

_____

_____

2. Start: From proteins, he made a treatment for glaucoma,
a disease that causes blindness.

Add: The proteins were soy.

Add: The treatment was chemical.

Add: The disease was of the eye.

Create: _____

_____

_____

_____

3. Start: He also found a way to make cortisone, a treatment
for people with arthritis.

Add: The way is inexpensive.

Add: The treatment is intermittent.

Create: _____

_____

_____

_____

Jeffrey was ~~happy~~ to meet the college basketball coach,

Mr. Harmon. Mr. Harmon seemed ~~happy~~ to meet Jeffrey

as well. Actually, he was ~~happy~~ to meet Jeffrey because Jeffrey

wanted to become part of his team. Jeffrey was known for his

slam dunks and for leaving the fans ~~happy~~.

10

(**PART B**) *Editing Your Paragraph*

Sound good?
Combine?
Omit?
Replace?
Expand?

a. As you read the paragraph aloud, ask yourself, "Does it **sound good**?"

b. **Replace** the underlined word in sentence 1 with a new word choice.

c. **Combine** sentences 2 and 3.

d. **Omit** an unnecessary word in sentence 4. (Make an X.)

e. **Combine** sentences 5, 6, and 7.

¹My grandfather was one of the <u>happiest</u> people I had ever met.

²He always had words for everyone. ³His words were kind. ⁴He

would say "hello" and smile as if I were the most were wonderful

person in his life. ⁵He took me on many adventures to see things.

⁶The adventures were interesting. ⁷The things were new.

Edited paragraph:

_____

_____

_____

_____

_____

_____

_____

_____

_____

_____

_____

PART A   *Sharpening Your Word Choices*

Nothing was right at the picnic. First, the weather was

~~terrible~~. It rained all day, and we never saw a ray of sunshine.

In addition, all that rain made the food soggy. The food was

~~terrible~~. Even the picnic area was ~~terrible~~. Garbage was

scattered everywhere. I was relieved when the picnic was over!

PART B   *Polishing Your Sentences (Sentence Expanding)*

1. Start: My favorite activity of the summer was a roller
            coaster ride.

   Add: Your own word or words that describe a summer
            that went on and on.

   Create: _____

   _____

   _____

2. Start: The roller coaster had a long series of drops.

Add: Your own word or words that describe the long series of drops that left someone's heart pounding.

Create: _____

_____

_____

3. Start: Every time we dropped, my brother closed his eyes and screamed.

Add: Your own word or words that describe the brother who was scared.

Create: _____

_____

_____

4. Start: Being the brother, I assured him of our safety.

Add: Your own word or words that describe the brother who was not scared.

Create: _____

_____

_____

PART A *Sharpening Your Word Choices*

Help Book
15

As usual, the clowns were the funniest circus act. Two

clowns were especially ~~funny~~. Even though they wore

simple black suits, their miming was ~~funny~~. Three other

clowns, dressed in ~~funny~~ costumes, performed a ~~funny~~ skit.

Before the act was over, everyone in the front row was

soaking wet.

PART B *Polishing Your Sentences (Sentence Expanding)*

1. Start: The chorus was preparing for a concert.

Add: Your own word or words that describe what kind of chorus.

Add: Your own word or words that describe which concert.

Create: _____

_____

_____

2. Start: Mr. Cline, our music director, rehearsed with us for weeks.

   Add: Your own word or words that describe how good the
   music director was.

   Add: Your own word or words that describe how many
   weeks they rehearsed.

   Create: _____

   _____

   _____

3. Start: At first, the songs did not sound like music.

   Add: Your own word or words that describe what kind of songs.

   Create: _____

   _____

   _____

4. Start: But as we practiced, music began to fill the hallways.

   Add: Your own word or words that describe how good the music was.

   Add: Your own word or words that describe what kind of hallways.

   Create: _____

   _____

   _____

PART A *Sharpening Your Word Choices*

In the 1800s, half of all surgical patients died from infection. The prospect of surgery was frightening! The ~~dirty~~ conditions in the hospitals led to all this infection and death. Even the operating rooms were very dirty places. In those days, surgeons did not wear masks or gloves. Surgeons rarely washed their ~~dirty~~ hands. Their ~~dirty~~ clothes were often covered in blood.

PART B *Polishing Your Sentences (Sentence Expanding)*

1. Start: Joseph Lister, a surgeon in the 1800s, was instrumental in changing the hospital procedures.

     Add: Your own word or words that describe a surgeon who knows a lot.

     Add: Your own word or words that describe hospital procedures that were very bad.

     Create: _____

_____

_____

2. Start: Doctors had to wear clothing and use instruments.

Add: Your own word or words that describe clothing that was not dirty.

Add: Your own words or words that describe instruments that were very, very clean.

Create: _____

_____

_____

3. Start: These procedures led to conditions that saved lives.

Add: Your own word or words that describe procedures that helped people.

Add: Your own word or words that describe conditions that saved lives.

Create: _____

_____

_____

Harriet Tubman was a ~~wonderful~~ woman. As a child,

she was a slave in the South. After she escaped to the

North, she wanted others to have the ~~wonderful~~ experience

of freedom also. Working with a ~~wonderful~~ group of people,

she helped many others in the South escape slavery. Harriet

Tubman and her ~~wonderful~~ acts of courage will never

be forgotten.

PART B   *Polishing Your Sentences (Sentence Expanding)*

1. Start: On December 1, 1955, Rosa Parks stepped onto a bus after a day of work.

     Add: Your own word or words that describe Rosa Parks after a long day of work.

     Add: Your own word or words that describe the kind of bus.

     Add: Your own word or words that describe what kind of day made her so tired.

     Create: _____

_____

_____

_____

2. Start: Parks was tired of the treatment of African Americans.

     Add: Your own word or words that describe treatment that was not nice.

     Create: _____

_____

_____

3. Start: When asked to give up her seat on the bus, this woman refused.

Add: Your own word or words that describe a woman who was willing to stand up for herself.

Create: _____

_____

_____

_____

4. Start: This act led to changes in U.S. laws concerning segregation.

Add: Your own word or words that describe an act that Rosa Parks took that was very good.

Add: Your own word or words that describe changes that were very good.

Create: _____

_____

_____

_____

(**PART A**) *Sharpening Your Word Choices*

The Wright Brothers must have been a little ~~scared~~

when they arrived at Kitty Hawk on December 17, 1903.

For years, they had carefully studied flight and conducted

many experiments. They were ready to test their power-driven

aircraft. Orville must have been ~~scared~~ as he lay down beside

the motor on the lower wing of the craft. His ~~scared~~ brother,

Wilbur, stayed on the ground. The first flight lasted only 12

seconds, but it was a great step forward in the history of flight.

PART B) *Editing Your Paragraph*

Sound good?
Combine?
Omit?
Replace?
Expand?

a. As you read the paragraph aloud, ask yourself, "Does it **sound good?**"

b. **Combine** sentences 1 and 2.

c. **Replace** the underlined word in sentence 4 with a new word choice.

d. **Combine** sentences 3, 4, and 5.

e. **Replace** the underlined word in sentence 7 with a new word choice.

f. **Combine** sentences 6, 7, and 8.

g. **Combine** sentences 9, 10, and 11.

h. **Expand** sentence 12 with one or two adjectives that describe the buttons on the stole.

¹Margaret wanted an outfit for the dance. ²It had to be perfect.

³After trips to many stores, she selected a formal. ⁴The formal was underlined pretty. ⁵The formal was white. ⁶The skirt of the formal was made of chiffon. ⁷The chiffon was underlined pretty. ⁸The chiffon was delicate.

⁹Margaret added a stole to the outfit. ¹⁰The stole was apricot.

¹¹The stole was beaded. ¹²The stole had buttons.

Edited paragraph:

_____

_____

_____

_____

_____

_____

_____

_____

_____

_____

Help Book
62

In choosing a future job, you should consider your talents and interests. Maybe your career will be in computers as ~~someone who programs software~~ or as ~~someone who designs graphics~~. If you like working with your hands, you might want to be ~~someone who works on houses~~ or ~~someone who makes clothing~~. If you really enjoy people, you might consider a health profession. You might choose to be ~~someone who gives medicine to people~~ or ~~someone who helps people make nutritional food choices~~. You can choose from so many great professions!

CAUTION AHEAD

DETOUR

p. 212

PART B *Polishing Your Sentences (Sentence Combining)*

1. Start: Traffic came to a standstill.

   Add: It was in front of the bus.

   Create: _____

   _____

   _____

2. Start: The bus driver sighed when she saw cars and trucks.

   Add: They were in the intersection.

   Create: _____

   _____

   _____

3. Start: "Just another traffic jam," she said to a passenger.

Add: The passenger was near the door.

Create: _____

_____

_____

4. Start: "It's a real problem."

Add: The real problem is in this city.

Create: _____

_____

_____

PART A *Sharpening Your Word Choices*

A ~~group of people~~ gathered to watch the track meet. The fans waited eagerly for the ~~people who compete~~ to enter the stadium. When it came to track and field, these fans were ~~people who know a lot~~. They couldn't wait to see who the ~~people who win~~ would be. The ~~young people~~ in the group grew restless. It didn't matter to them who the ~~people who win~~ were.

PART B *Polishing Your Sentences (Sentence Combining)*

1. Start: Sara's bus broke down.

Add: It broke down on the freeway.

Add: It broke down near the arena.

Create: _____

_____

_____

_____

2. Start: A tow truck pulled the bus.

Add: The tow truck went to the garage.

Add: The garage was across town.

Create: _____

_____

_____

3. Start: The mechanics examined the suspension.

Add: The suspension was under the bus.

Add: The mechanics were in the garage.

Create: _____

_____

_____

4. Start: However, they determined that the problem was the axle.

Add: The axle is between the back tires.

Create: _____

_____

_____

_____

PART A   *Sharpening Your Word Choices*

You can find many housing options in urban areas.

Some people purchase single family dwellings, including

~~homes that can be moved~~, ~~small houses~~, and ~~large houses~~.

On the other hand, many city dwellers prefer to live in buildings

with other families. For example, two families might live in

a ~~building with two homes~~. Or, several families might live in

~~buildings with many homes~~.

PART B   *Polishing Your Sentences (Sentence Expanding)*

1. Start: A mouse was loose.

    Add: Your own words that tell *where* the mouse was loose.

    Add: Your own word or words that describe the mouse.

    Create: _____

    _____

    _____

Help Book 53

Help Book 81

18

2. Start: Sheldon suspected that the mouse had a home.

Add: Your own words that tell *where* the mouse's home was.

Create: _____

_____

_____

Help Book 81

3. Start: Sheldon and his sister, Amy, saw it run.

Add: Your own word or words that describe Sheldon's sister.

Add: Your own words that tell *where* the mouse ran.

Create: _____

_____

_____

4. Start: Amy screamed when the mouse scurried.

Add: Your own words that tell *where* the mouse scurried.

Create: _____

_____

_____

PART A *Sharpening Your Word Choices*

Last summer, I spent a peaceful week camping in

a ~~place with lots of trees~~. My campsite was right next to

a ~~place with some water~~, so I had fresh water for cooking and

bathing. Each day, I took a short hike. On the first day, I

followed the water until I found a ~~place with grass~~ full of

wildflowers. It was so beautiful that I returned many times. I

saved the most challenging hike for the last day. I hiked until

I came to the base of a steep ~~place~~. I climbed to the top and

discovered a breathtaking view of a wide ~~place~~.

PART B *Polishing Your Sentences (Sentence Expanding)*

1. Start: A pioneer family settled.

　　Add: Your own words that tell *where* they settled.

　　Create: _____

_____

Help Book
81

2. Start: The first thing they did was to build a cabin.

   Add: Your own words that tell *where* they built their cabin.

   Add: Your own word or words that describe the cabin.

   Create: _____

   _____

   _____

3. Start: The family constructed the cabin out of logs.

   Add: Your own words that tell *where* the logs came from.

   Create: _____

   _____

   _____

4. Start: They filled the cracks with moss and clay.

   Add: Your own words that tell *where* the cracks were.

   Create: _____

   _____

   _____

PART A · *Sharpening Your Word Choices*

Mr. Hill's boss generously offered the use of his condominium

in the Florida Keys for two weeks. To make the most of this

vacation offer, the Hill children needed new ~~clothes~~. Alex, the

six-year old, needed ~~pants~~, ~~shirts~~, and ~~shoes~~. Ben, the oldest

boy, needed one pair of ~~pants~~, ~~shirts~~ in two colors, and ~~shoes~~.

Beth, the thirteen-year old, wanted some ~~pants~~ for the beach

and ~~something to wear if the weather was cool~~.

20

Sound good?
Combine?
Omit?
Replace?
Expand?

a. As you read the paragraph aloud, ask yourself, "Does it **sound good**?"

b. **Combine** sentences 1 and 2.

c. **Combine** sentences 3 and 4.

d. **Omit** a word that's unnecessary or doesn't sound good in sentence 5. (Make an X.)

e. **Replace** the underlined word in sentence 5 with a new word choice.

f. **Expand** by adding words in sentence 6 that tell *where* the women hang their clothes to dry.

¹Women in villages do not have washing machines. ²The villages are in the jungle. ³The women wash their clothes by hand. ⁴They wash them in a stream. ⁵They place the skirt or robe on a large, gigantic, smooth rock and then scrub it with a <u>little</u> wooden paddle. ⁶Then they hang their clothes to dry.

Edited paragraph:

_____

_____

_____

_____

_____

_____

_____

_____

_____

PART A   *Sharpening Your Word Choices*

Tyrone couldn't wait to go to Riviera Maya in Mexico. He

drove his ~~car~~ to the Miami airport. On the way, he carefully

maneuvered around dozens of ~~large trucks~~ and ~~small trucks~~

and hoped he wouldn't be late. When he arrived at the airport,

he jumped out of his car and raced to the gate. Once he was

comfortably seated on the ~~aircraft~~ that would fly him to Cancun,

he thought about the ~~vehicle~~ he would drive to the beach. What

a great vacation!

PART B *Polishing Your Sentences (Sentence Combining)*

1. Start: Maria traveled to her aunt's for a vacation.

Add: She went in early summer.

Create: _____

_____

_____

_____

2. Start: They often went to the beach.

Add: They went after breakfast.

Add: They went to swim.

Create: _____

_____

_____

_____

3. Start: They usually ate lunch.

Add: They ate about noon.

Add: They ate at the Beach Café.

Create: _____

_____

_____

_____

_____

4. Start: Maria and her aunt would play cards.

Add: They would play after lunch.

Add: They would sit on a blanket.

Add: They played until they had enough sun.

Create: _____

_____

_____

_____

_____

(**PART A**) *Sharpening Your Word Choices*

For many years, Christina had dreamed of going on an

African safari. Filled with excitement, she read the guidebook.

She wouldn't be allowed to carry many ~~things~~. She should bring

sturdy boots, of course, but not her ~~jewelry~~. Christina was

relieved to learn that she wouldn't need foreign ~~money~~ and that

the safari staff would be bringing all the ~~food~~. Christina was

thrilled that she could put all her attention before the trip on

choosing a new digital zoom camera.

22

1. Start: Jared has many things to do.

Add: He has to do them before the new school year begins.

Create: _____

_____

_____

_____

2. Start: He will finish shopping for school supplies.

Add: He will shop this afternoon.

Add: He will shop at the mall.

Create: _____

_____

_____

_____

3. Start: He will check his list.

Add: He will check it tonight.

Add: He will check it before he goes to bed.

Create: _____

_____

_____

_____

_____

23

How do people keep someone else from copying their work and claiming the credit themselves? Copyright laws protect things that people create. For example, composers use copyright laws to prevent their ~~music~~ from being copied without permission. Artists make sure that someone else does not claim their ~~art~~. Authors copyright their ~~stories~~ to prevent others from copying the stories and selling them. Even writers for magazines use copyrights to protect articles about all kinds of topics, from ~~gardens~~ to ~~meals~~ to ~~shows~~.

1. Start: The Hotel Regent provides three meals to its guests.

Add: Your own words that tell *when* the meals are provided.

Add: Your own word or words that describe the meals.

Create: _____

_____

_____

2. Start: Guests may help themselves to breakfast.

Add: Your own words that tell *when*.

Add: Your own words that tell *where*.

Create: _____

_____

_____

23

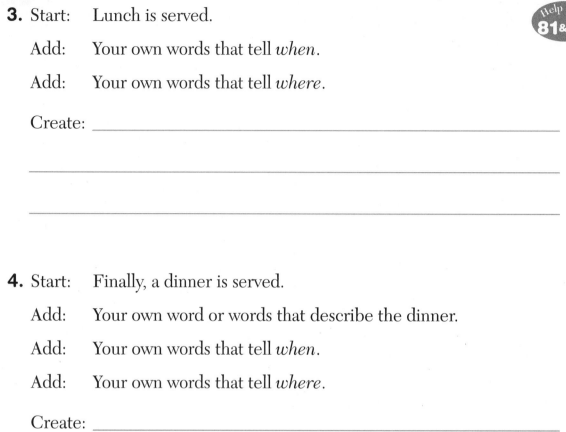

3. Start: Lunch is served.

Add: Your own words that tell *when*.

Add: Your own words that tell *where*.

Create: _____

_____

_____

4. Start: Finally, a dinner is served.

Add: Your own word or words that describe the dinner.

Add: Your own words that tell *when*.

Add: Your own words that tell *where*.

Create: _____

_____

_____

Help Book
81&82

PART A   *Sharpening Your Word Choices*

For many years, Italy's Mount Etna had threatened to erupt

again. In 2001, Italy experienced the ~~beginning~~ of a series of

eruptions. Lava poured out of Etna and down its sides. Hundreds

of earthquakes marked the ~~beginning~~ of months of volcanic

activity. Along with these ~~events~~, scientists observed a lava

fountain that rose more than 1,000 feet above the volcano. The

mountain's eruption could have been a ~~disaster~~, but nobody was

hurt and there was little damage.

PART B   *Polishing Your Sentences (Sentence Expanding)*

1. Start: The state's two best football teams met.

     Add: Your own words that tell *when*.

     Add: Your own words that tell *where*.

     Create: _____

_____

_____

24

2. Start: 3,000 fans began filling the stands.

Add: Your own words that tell *when*.

Add: Your own word or words that describe the fans.

Create: _____

_____

3. Start: The game ended when Jon Hanson threw a 50-yard pass.

Add: Your own word or words that describe the game.

Add: Your own words that tell *where* Jon threw the pass.

Create: _____

_____

_____

4. Start: Coach Gomez thanked the team for their effort.

Add: Your own words that tell *where* Coach Gomez
            thanked the team.

Add: Your own words that tell *when* Coach Gomez
            thanked the team.

Add: Your own word or words that describe the team's effort.

Create: _____

_____

_____

_____

PART A   *Sharpening Your Word Choices*

The limbic system is the part of the brain that controls

emotions and our responses to danger. When we feel fear, the

limbic system tells us to defend ourselves or run away. Emotions,

such as ~~love~~, hate, ~~feeling sad~~, ~~being mad~~, and ~~being happy~~, also

originate from the limbic system. The limbic system remembers

when we felt ~~an excited feeling~~ or ~~a calm feeling~~ in the past.

When something like a smell or a sound reminds us of those

times, we experience the same emotions again.

(**PART B**) *Editing Your Paragraph*

Sound good?
Combine?
Omit?
Replace?
Expand?

a.   As you read the paragraph aloud, ask yourself, "Does it **sound good?**"

b.   **Combine** sentences 1, 2, and 3.

c.   **Combine** sentences 4 and 5.

d.   **Omit** a word that's unnecessary or doesn't sound good in sentence 7. (Make an X.)

e.   **Replace** the underlined word in sentence 8 with a new word choice.

¹Your brain sends messages. ²They go to your body. ³This happens when feeling strong emotions. ⁴For example, your heart may beat faster. ⁵It beats faster when you become angry. ⁶If you're scared, the pupils of your eyes may dilate. ⁷Also, extra blood flows to your muscles, too. ⁸Even pleasant emotions, such as <u>happiness</u>, can have this effect.

Edited paragraph:

_____

_____

_____

_____

_____

_____

_____

_____

_____

The crafts class offers many options from which to select.

Many people choose to ~~make~~ clay pots and bowls. Some people

use the large collection of colorful beads to ~~make~~ beaded jewelry.

Other people ~~make~~ collages from small pieces of tile and

broken dishes. Finally, a few people like to draw or paint.

What would you ~~make~~?

PART B *Polishing Your Sentences (Sentence Combining)*

1. Start: José learned about different breeds of dogs.

   Add: Jenny learned about different breeds of dogs.

   Add: Marcus learned about different breeds of dogs.

   Create: _____

   _____

   _____

2. Start: Dachshunds are a hound breed.

   Add: Greyhounds are a hound breed.

   Add: Beagles are a hound breed.

   Create: _____

   _____

   _____

3. Start: Pekingese are a type of toy dog.

Add: Toy poodles are a type of toy dog.

Add: Pugs are a type of toy dog.

Create: _____

_____

_____

4. Start: Sporting dogs include cocker spaniels.

Add: Sporting dogs include golden retrievers.

Add: Sporting dogs include Irish setters.

Create: _____

_____

_____

PART A *Sharpening Your Word Choices*

Recently, Geoff and Nola visited the Australia Museum. They ~~liked~~ the variety of exhibits. Geoff particularly liked the insect displays, which included termites, cockroaches, and beetles. Nola ~~liked~~ the Chapman Mineral Collection. It contained over 800 outstanding specimens. Geoff and Nola both ~~liked~~ the exhibition that explored the lives of indigenous Australians.

PART B *Polishing Your Sentences (Sentence Combining)*

1. Start: On Jake's 100ᵗʰ birthday, his children gathered to celebrate.

　　Add: His grandchildren gathered to celebrate.

　　Add: His great grandchildren gathered to celebrate.

　　Create: _____

　　_____

　　_____

2. Start: They surprised him with gifts.

Add: They surprised him with cards.

Create: _____

_____

_____

3. Start: Everyone ate chocolate birthday cake.

Add: Everyone ate vanilla ice cream.

Add: Everyone ate candy.

Create: _____

_____

_____

4. Start: Jake enjoyed the party.

Add: His family enjoyed the party.

Create: _____

_____

_____

PART A *Sharpening Your Word Choices*

People from many age groups joined the United Way

Walkathon. A pack of Cub Scouts ~~walked~~ down the street,

carrying a large banner. Three teenage girls ~~walked~~ aimlessly,

exchanging school gossip. An older couple ~~walked~~ along, waving

and smiling at their friends. At the back of the group, a tiny

three-year old ~~walked~~ while her parents patiently pressed onward.

PART B *Polishing Your Sentences (Sentence Combining)*

1. Start: The children hurried to the gymnasium.

Add: The children sat down.

Create: _____

_____

_____

2. Start: They were excited to see the play.

Add: They were excited to meet the actors.

Create: _____

_____

_____

3. Start: They sat quietly.

Add: They listened to the story.

Add: They laughed.

Create: _____

_____

_____

4. Start: At the end, they stood up.

Add: At the end, they broke into loud applause.

Create: _____

_____

_____

PART A *Sharpening Your Word Choices*

Four people entered the ten-minute shopping competition.

When the bell went off, Lee ~~ran~~ to the canned foods to stock up.

Margaret ~~ran~~ to get disposable diapers for her babies. Paul

~~ran~~ down the middle aisle to the frozen food section. The winner,

Rebecca, ~~ran~~ to the meat department for the highest priced

items in the store.

PART B *Polishing Your Sentences (Sentence Combining)*

1. Start: Children have always rolled wooden or metal hoops.

Add: Children have always thrown wooden or metal hoops.

Add: Children have always twirled wooden or metal hoops.

Create: _____

_____

_____

2. Start: Then, in 1957, Richard Knerr developed a hoop made of hollow plastic.

Add: Arthur Melin developed the hoop made of plastic, too.

Create: _____

_____

_____

_____

3. Start: Knerr and Melin gave the new toy the name "hula hoop."

Add: Knerr and Melin manufactured millions of them.

Add: Knerr and Melin sold 25 million in just two months.

Create: _____

_____

_____

_____

PART A *Sharpening Your Word Choices*

In large cities like Chicago, you could easily experience the

foods of many countries in one evening. First, you could stop at

a small restaurant to ~~eat~~ Chinese delicacies known as dim sum.

Then, you could ~~eat~~ at an Italian restaurant where ravioli with

meat sauce is a favorite. Finally, you could ~~eat~~ dessert at a

French restaurant where many people order crepes with

cheese or fruit filling.

(**PART B**) *Editing Your Paragraph*

Sound good?
Combine?
Omit?
Replace?
Expand?

a. As you read the paragraph aloud, ask yourself, "Does it **sound good**?"

b. **Combine** sentences 1 and 2.

c. **Combine** sentences 5 and 6.

d. **Combine** sentences 7, 8, and 9.

e. **Combine** sentences 10, 11, and 12.

f. **Replace** the underlined word in sentence 13 with a new word choice.

g. **Combine** sentences 13 and 14.

¹Many species of bats catch their food. ²They catch their food while flying. ³But, bats are not birds. ⁴Bats are the only mammals that fly. ⁵Bats are quite efficient at catching food. ⁶They catch it in a short amount of time. ⁷For example, the brown bat catches up to 1,200 night-flying insects. ⁸They catch them in one hour.

⁹The brown bat is little. ¹⁰The little brown bat enjoys flies.

¹¹The little brown bat enjoys wasps. ¹²It enjoys moths, too.

¹³The bat goes home for the night and <u>eats</u> its food.

¹⁴It goes home after putting that many insects into its mouth.

Edited paragraph:

_____

_____

_____

_____

_____

_____

_____

_____

_____

_____

_____

_____

_____

_____

At Jefferson Middle School, teachers acknowledge students' good behavior every day. However, teachers also give consequences for inappropriate behavior. If a student ~~takes~~ drugs or weapons to school, school officials ~~take~~ the items and recommend suspension. If a student ~~takes~~ school property, the case is turned over to the police. On the other hand, if a student takes someone's lunch, the lunch monitor assigns detention.

PART B *Polishing Your Sentences (Sentence Combining)*

1. Start: Linda grabbed a seat.

Add: Bobby grabbed a seat.

Add: The seats were adjoining.

Add: The seats were on the bus.

Add: The bus was crowded.

Create: _____

_____

_____

2. Start: They had just seen a movie.

Add: They had taken a tour.

Add: They had been at the National Air and Space Museum.

Create: _____

_____

_____

3. Start: They were really tired.

Add: They were tired after all that activity.

Create: _____

_____

32

PART A   *Sharpening Your Word Choices*

Last year, our garden was a disappointment. But, this year, we had an incredible garden. We planted sun-loving vegetables in an area with no shade. To encourage the plants to ~~grow~~, we supplied them with plenty of water and fertilizer. We mulched and weeded and thinned the plants. The tomatoes, beans, squash, and beets ~~grew~~. Unlike the year before, the harvest ~~grew~~ beyond our expectations.

PART B   *Polishing Your Sentences (Sentence Combining)*

1. Start: Giraffes are animals.

   Add: The animals are fascinating.

   Create: _____

   _____

2. Start: (Some) giraffes weigh as much as 4,000 pounds.

   Add: The giraffes are male.

   Add: They grow to be 18 feet tall.

   Add: They have necks that are 7 feet long.

   Create: _____

_____

_____

_____

3. Start: Female giraffes do not weigh as much as males.

   Add: Baby giraffes do not weigh as much as males.

   Add: Female giraffes are not as tall as males.

   Add: Baby giraffes are not as tall as males.

   Create: _____

_____

_____

_____

PART A   *Sharpening Your Word Choices*

Rob Garrison collects classic Fords. The first classic car he ~~got~~ was a blue 1965 Mustang. Then he ~~got~~ a pink and white 1955 Ford Crown Victoria with a Plexiglas top. He sold that car to ~~get~~ a 1957 Ford Skyliner with a black interior. Finally, he flew to New York to ~~get~~ a 1956 Ford Sunliner convertible, a classic with such beautiful styling that he still owns it today.

PART B   *Polishing Your Sentences (Sentence Combining)*

1. Start: King Khufu (or Cheops) built the pyramid.

   Add: The pyramid was the greatest.

   Add: The pyramid was built in Egypt.

   Add: The pyramid was built around 2600 BC.

   Create: _____

   _____

   _____

33

2. Start: The Great Pyramid is the oldest of the Seven
            Wonders of the Ancient World.

Add: The Great Pyramid remains standing.

Add: It remains standing today.

Create: _____

_____

_____

_____

3. Start: Workers used blocks to build the pyramid.

Add: Workers used two million blocks.

Add: The blocks were limestone.

Create: _____

_____

_____

As soon as summer arrived, Erica ~~went~~ for her long-delayed

vacation. She ~~went~~ to Europe by plane. First, she ~~went~~ to Paris,

which is her favorite city. Then, she ~~went~~ to Prague where she

met three friends. The four of them ~~went~~ to Berlin before they

~~went~~ back to the United States. After five exciting weeks in

Europe, Erica immediately began dreaming about her next

vacation.

PART B *Polishing Your Sentences (Sentence Combining)*

1. Start: Charlie visited historic Fort Clatsop.

   Add: His nephew visited historic Fort Clatsop, too.

   Add: Fort Clatsop is in Oregon.

   Create: _____

   _____

   _____

2. Start: They learned about the adventures of the Lewis and Clark Expedition.

   Add: The adventures were fantastic.

   Create: _____

   _____

   _____

3. Start: They explored the abandoned canoe landing.

Add: They toured the fort replica.

Add: They learned how the members of the Expedition boiled seawater to make salt.

Create: _____

_____

_____

_____

_____

PART A   *Sharpening Your Word Choices*

Police detectives are trained to be very observant when

investigating a crime. When they arrive at a crime scene, they

~~look at~~ it very systematically. Highly trained detectives carefully

~~look at~~ every square inch for evidence. Unlike the rest of us, they

see meaning in the smallest things. If they ~~see~~ even a tiny fiber

from a wool sweater, it might unravel the mystery.

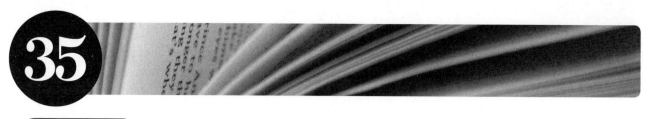

35

PART B *Editing Your Paragraph*

Sound good?
Combine?
Omit?
Replace?
Expand?

a. As you read the paragraph aloud, ask yourself, "Does it **sound good**?"

b. **Combine** sentences 1, 2, 3, and 4.

c. **Combine** sentences 5 and 6.

d. **Replace** the underlined word in sentence 5 with a new word choice.

e. **Combine** sentences 7 and 8.

f. **Combine** sentences 9 and 10.

¹Edwin Binney established the company that now makes Crayola Crayons. ²Harold Smith established the company, too. ³They established the company in the late 1800s. ⁴They established the company in New York City. ⁵At first, Binney & Smith <u>made</u> slate pencils for students. ⁶They also made dustless chalk for teachers. ⁷They toured schools and noticed that children needed inexpensive crayons. ⁸They toured schools after receiving a gold medal for the dustless chalk. ⁹They created the first eight colors that you can still buy today. ¹⁰They created the eight colors in 1903. ¹¹By 1996, Binney & Smith had produced 100 billion crayons.

Edited paragraph:

_____

_____

_____

_____

_____

_____

_____

_____

_____

_____

_____

_____

_____

Through careful observation, we ~~know~~ more and more about

sea turtles. We ~~know~~ that they are unusual animals. Although

they live in the ocean and can swim long distances, they must

come to the surface to breathe. Female sea turtles must also

venture onto the land to lay their eggs. We ~~know~~ what a

difficult task coming ashore is because we know their bodies

are designed for life in the water, not on land.

PART B *Polishing Your Sentences (Sentence Combining)*

Topic Sentence: Giraffes have many unique physical characteristics.

1. Start: They are the largest of the cud-chewing animals _____.

　　 Add: One of the following, using parallel structure.

　　　　 • and live in Africa

　　　　 • and the tallest mammal on Earth

　　 Create: _____

_____

_____

2. Start: Both female and male giraffes have very long necks, smooth horns _____.

　　 Add: Three of the following, using parallel structure.

　　　　 • and eat foliage

　　　　 • and high shoulders

　　　　 • and long legs

　　　　 • and short manes

　　　　 • and spend nearly one-half of their day eating

　　 Create: _____

_____

_____

_____

3. Start: The male giraffes weigh 2,420 to 4,250 pounds _____.

   Add: Two of the following, using parallel structure.

- and are 18 feet in height

- and spend 22% of their day walking

- and have thick horns

Create: _____

_____

_____

_____

4. Start: The females, on the other hand, weigh a third less _____.

   Add: Two of the following, using parallel structure.

- and are two feet shorter

- and take care of their babies

- and have thinner horns than males

Create: _____

_____

_____

_____

(**PART A**)   *Sharpening Your Word Choices*

Artists ~~use~~ many tools in their work. For example, a visual

artist may ~~use~~ a variety of paint brushes or palette knives. Some

begin with brushes that are rather coarse and then ~~use~~ thin, fine

brushes for details. A sculptor may use a hammer and chisels and

then finish with sandpaper. Some artists ~~use~~ power tools, personal

computers, or lasers. Artists choose their tools according to their

tastes and the art they want to create.

**CAUTION
AHEAD**

DETOUR

p. 217

PART B *Polishing Your Sentences (Sentence Combining)*

Topic Sentence: The giraffe's physical features affect how it moves.

1. Start: The giraffe has two gaits (ways of moving), a walk _____ .

   Add: One of the following, using parallel structure.

   • and galloping

   • and a gallop

   Create: _____

   _____

   _____

2. Start: A giraffe's long legs _____ result in an ambling walk.

   Add: One of the following, using parallel structure.

   • and short body

   • and has a short body

   Create: _____

   _____

   _____

3. Start: The giraffe supports its weight alternately, first on both left legs _____, just as a camel walks.

Add: One of the following, using parallel structure.

- and then on both right legs

- and then with right legs

Create: _____

_____

_____

_____

4. Start: However, when a giraffe gallops, it uses pairs of forelegs _____, just as a rabbit runs.

Add: One of the following, using parallel structure.

- and hind legs

- and those hind legs

Create: _____

_____

_____

_____

38

The city of Lake Frances ~~gave~~ Mark Howell a plaque for his many years of service. Mark generously ~~gave~~ his time and energy, as well as his considerable wealth, to many local causes. Mark ~~gave~~ a great deal of money to community agencies. For example, he gave school supplies to hundreds of children each fall. In addition, Mark ~~gave~~ land for construction of a shelter for people who are homeless. He also funded a performing arts center.

PART B *Polishing Your Sentences (Sentence Combining)*

Topic Sentence: The giraffe's method of eating is quite different from most animals.

1. Start: The giraffe's narrow muzzle _____
enable it to eat leaves from hard-to-reach places.

Add: Two of the following, using parallel structure.

- and flexible upper lip

- and are able to move their lips

- and long tongue

Create: _____

_____

_____

_____

2. Start: They feed on leaves at the tops of tall deciduous
trees, including Acacia _____.

Add: One of the following, using parallel structure.

- and Combretum

- and eat Combretum foliage

Create: _____

_____

_____

_____

3. Start: Giraffes get plenty of water from the leaves
they eat _____ .

Add: One of the following, using parallel structure.

- and can go two to three days without finding
another water source

- and two to three days without finding another
water source

Create: _____

_____

_____

_____

PART A *Sharpening Your Word Choices*

If you want to build a structure on public or private land, the city must decide if it will ~~let~~ you construct the building. An employee of the city planning office must review your plans. In some cases, the city will not ~~let~~ you proceed without making major changes in the plans. If you have followed all regulations, the city ~~lets~~ you put up the building. Finally, with the permit in hand, you may begin your project.

(**PART B**) *Polishing Your Sentences (Sentence Combining)*

Topic Sentence: Giraffe herds differ from those of many other animals.

1. Start: Male, female _____ do not stay together in a single herd.

Add: One of the following, using parallel structure.

- and live together as a group

- and giraffe herds

- and young giraffes

Create: _____

_____

_____

2. Start: One or more female giraffes _____ form family herds.

Add: One of the following, using parallel structure.

- and their family herds

- and eat too many leaves

- and their young

Create: _____

_____

_____

3. Start: As they grow older, young males leave _____ while females stay for life.

Add: One of the following, using parallel structure.

- and all-male herds

- and join all-male herds

- and looking for water

Create: _____

_____

_____

_____

(**PART A**)   *Sharpening Your Word Choices*

When Mrs. Jones ~~said~~, "It is time for class to begin," a

nervous silence fell upon the class.

Paula leaned over to Robert and ~~said~~, "Are you ready for

the test?"

"Test!" Robert ~~said~~. "What test?"

"The final social studies test," she said with surprise.

She couldn't believe that Robert had completely forgotten

about the test.

PART B *Editing Your Paragraph*

Sound good?
Combine?
Omit?
Replace?
Expand?

a. As you read the paragraph aloud, ask yourself, "Does it **sound good**?"

b. **Combine** sentences 1 and 2.

c. **Combine** sentences 3 and 4.

d. **Combine** sentences 5 and 6.

e. **Replace** the underlined word in sentence 5.

f. **Expand** sentence 7 by telling what else is needed to become good at origami.

g. **Omit** a word that's unnecessary or doesn't sound good in sentence 8. (Make an X.)

h. **Combine** sentences 8 and 9.

¹Origami is an art form. ²The art form is Japanese. ³It involves folding paper into shapes. ⁴The shapes are three-dimensional. ⁵You could <u>make</u> origami butterflies and cranes. ⁶You could make origami frogs and dogs. ⁷It takes patience to master the art of origami. ⁸Today, origami is mostly mainly used for decorating at parties. ⁹Origami is mainly used for decorating at special events.

Edited paragraph:

_____

_____

_____

_____

_____

_____

_____

_____

_____

PART A *Sharpening Your Word Choices*

Of all the students at Jackson School, Rob had the largest

collection of baseball cards. He ~~had~~ almost 900 cards, which he

~~had~~ in special plastic envelopes. He bought packs of cards that

~~had~~ three to fifteen cards each. The excitement of opening each

pack was to find out if it ~~had~~ a valuable card. Not all packs did.

Rob's most prized item was an Alex Rodriguez card, which was

priced in 2006 at $225.

(PART B) *Polishing Your Sentences (Sentence Combining)*

Topic Sentence: Rob is broke.

1. Start: He *either* has to find a part-time job _____.

Add: One of the following, using a phrase that makes sense.

- or sell his collection of baseball cards

- or buy another box for his cards

- or go get something to eat

Create: _____

_____

_____

2. Start: He could work at the ice cream shop _____.

Add: One of the following, using a phrase that makes sense.

- or eat too much

- or his parents would drive him there

- or deliver papers before school

Create: _____

_____

_____

3. Start: He could sell half of his card collection for
$500 _____.

Add: One of the following, using a phrase that makes sense.

- or buy more cards

- or his friends could buy them

- or all of his cards for $1,000

Create: _____

_____

_____

4. Start: *Either* Rob's Willie Mays card _____
could sell for more than $75.

Add: One of the following, using a phrase that makes sense.

- or all of them

- or his Mickey Mantle card

- or the baseball cards

Create: _____

_____

_____

42

(**PART A**) *Sharpening Your Word Choices*

The Hmong are a tribe of people that have never had a

country of their own. In the 18th century, they migrated from

China and ~~lived~~ in Laos. Forced to leave Laos after the Vietnam

War, many Hmong had to ~~live~~ in refugee camps. Now many

Hmong ~~live~~ in the United States, particularly in California,

Minnesota, Wisconsin, North Carolina, Georgia, and Michigan.

In spite of having lived within many other societies, their own

culture has managed to ~~live~~.

PART B *Polishing Your Sentences (Sentence Combining)*

Topic Sentence: Marissa had many decisions to make about her upcoming vacation.

1. Start: She had to decide whether to ask her friend Beth _____ to travel with her.

Add: Two of the following, using phrases that make sense.

- or her older sister Amy

- or her sister Amy is older

- or her neighbor Cindy

- or by herself

Create: _____

_____

_____

_____

2. Start: She couldn't decide whether to go to California _____.

Add: Two of the following, using phrases that make sense.

- or Montana

- or not California

- or Arizona

- or invite friends along

Create: _____

_____

3. Start: Marissa had learned many fascinating things about Arizona in school _____.

Add: One of the following, using a phrase that makes sense.

- or had always wanted to visit the state

- and had always wanted to visit the state

- or studied California

Create: _____

_____

_____

_____

4. Start: On the other hand, it might be nice to stay at a local resort _____.

Add: One of the following, using a phrase that makes sense.

- and spend the whole vacation at home

- or spend a week at home

- or leave the resort on Saturday

- and begin the trip next week

Create: _____

_____

_____

_____

When the Wong family first got cable TV, Ann loved to

channel surf. One day, she clicked to a channel where two people

were ~~talking~~ about how to win a bicycle race. Then, she changed

to a talk show where a young man was ~~talking~~ about a significant

event in his life. On another channel, a TV personality ~~talked~~

about politics. Finally, Ann found a soap opera where an angry

mother ~~talked~~ to her daughter about watching too much TV. Ann

decided that it was time to turn off the TV and do something else.

43

Topic Sentence: Ben was thinking about which homework he would do before dinner and where he wanted to work.

1. Start: He could work on his history paper _____.

Add: Two of the following, using parallel structure.

- or do his algebra assignment

- or studying for his test

- or more health

- or read his science chapter

Create: _____

_____

_____

_____

2. Start: His history paper had to be about a civil war _____.

Add: One of the following, using parallel structure.

- or writing about a peace treaty

- or a peace treaty

- or 10 pages long

Create: _____

_____

_____

3. Start: Would it be better to work in his room _____?

   Add: One of the following, using parallel structure.

- or at the kitchen table

- and at the kitchen table

- or not today

- and music playing

Create: _____

_____

_____

Detective Trumble searched the room. He ~~found~~ that the telephone receiver was off the hook. He would ask someone to dust it for fingerprints. He inspected the victim and ~~found~~ powder burns near the bullet hole. Concluding that the victim was shot at close range, he scanned the room for signs of a struggle. Amazingly, he ~~found~~ a gun under the desk. "Wouldn't it be something if we ~~found~~ the murderer today!" he thought. Justice would be swift.

PART B *Polishing Your Sentences (Sentence Combining)*

Topic Sentence: You can use a bar graph to compare two or more sets of data.

1. Start: Bar graphs use shaded bars _____
   to represent different amounts.

   Add: One of the following, using parallel structure.

   - or another thing

   - or not colored

   - or colored strips

   Create: _____

   _____

   _____

2. Start: Bar graphs can be vertical _____.

   Add: One of the following, using parallel structure.

   - or horizontal

   - and horizontal

   - or a line graph

   - and another kind

   Create: _____

   _____

   _____

3. Start: Graphs help people immediately see _____ data.

Add: One of the following, using parallel structure.

- or to understand

- and understanding

- or quickly understand

- and quickly understand

Create: _____

_____

_____

Rules for Tutors:

1. Come on time.

2. ~~Stay~~ at your tutoring station while you are waiting for your client.

3. If your client is not on time, ~~stay~~ at least 15 minutes. If the client still has not come, you may leave.

4. Make notes every day on your client's progress.

5. Don't ~~stay~~ in the Tutoring Center if you are not waiting for or working with a client. It will distract those who are working.

45

PART B **PART B** *Editing Your Paragraph*

Sound good?
Combine?
Omit?
Replace?
Expand?

a. As you read the paragraph aloud, ask yourself, "Does it **sound good**?"

b. **Combine** sentences 1, 2, 3, 4, and 5.

c. **Combine** sentences 6, 7, and 8.

d. **Expand** by adding a word in sentence 8 that describes the Yangtze River.

e. **Replace** the underlined words in sentence 9 with two new words.

f. **Omit** the unnecessary words in sentence 9. (Make an X.)

g. **Combine** sentences 10 and 11.

¹Sam is taking a trip. ²His friends Jeff and Susan are taking a trip. ³They are going to China. ⁴China is exotic. ⁵The trip will be in April. ⁶The tour begins in Beijing. ⁷The tour ends in Hong Kong. ⁸The tour includes a three-day cruise down the Yangtze River. ⁹During the trip, they will stay in many <u>good</u> hotels and eat many <u>good</u> meals while on the trip. ¹⁰The threesome must choose whether to spend three days in Shanghai. ¹¹They must choose whether to spend three days in China's garden cities. ¹²Regardless of their choice, they know they will have a wonderful time.

Edited paragraph:

(PART A) *Sharpening Your Word Choices*

I ~~want~~ chocolate. I like most types, but I ~~want~~ a chocolate candy bar rather than a cup of hot chocolate. When my best friend and I go out on Friday nights, I ~~want~~ ice cream with chocolate sauce. When my parents promise to bring me back something from their vacation, I ~~want~~ chocolate-covered macadamia nuts. What can I say?! I ~~want~~ chocolate!

DETOUR p. 219

PART B *Polishing Your Sentences (Sentence Combining)*

Topic Sentence: In 1999, Nick Corirossi was the middle school winner in the National Children's Film Festival.

1. Start: Nick, who was 12 years old at the time, was happy with the recognition _____ .

Add: One of the following, using a phrase that makes sense.

- or did not want it to go to his head

- but did not want it to go to his head

- but has gone to his head

Create: _____

_____

_____

_____

2. Start: The movie he made, *Milton's 15 Minutes*, was his first movie _____.

Add: One of the following, using a phrase that makes sense.

- but not the movie of Milton

- but the first movie he ever made

- but not his last movie

Create: _____

_____

_____

3. Start: Since 1999, Nick has won awards for two
other movies _____.

Add: One of the following, using parallel structure.

- and loves to play baseball

- and he has two brothers

- and he will probably win more awards

Create: _____

_____

_____

_____

4. Start: Ever since he was 6 years old, Nick has been interested
in making real movies _____.

Add: One of the following, using a clause that makes sense.

- but he is not interested in acting

- or not interested in acting

- but not interested in acting the movies

Create: _____

_____

_____

_____

PART A *Sharpening Your Word Choices*

Ted went through the same routine every night. He would

~~put~~ his shoes on the floor by the dresser and ~~put~~ his shirt on

the chair near the door. Then, he would ~~put~~ the keys for his

bike, his locker, and the house on the table by his bed. Finally,

he would ~~put~~ his gum on the bedpost and hope that he would

remember it in the morning.

47

PART B *Polishing Your Sentences (Sentence Combining)*

Topic Sentence: People have always been fascinated by the moon.

1. Start: Across time, people have seen the moon _____.

Add: One of the following, using a phrase that makes sense.

- or walked on it

- but only recently by visiting it

- but looking at it

Create: _____

_____

_____

2. Start: If you were standing on the moon, you would see a
dark sky _____.

Add: One of the following, using a clause that makes sense.

- but you would not see clouds

- or you would see no clouds

- but no clouds to see

Create: _____

_____

_____

_____

3. Start: You would see no evidence of air, water _____ on the moon.

    Add: One of the following, using a phrase that makes sense.

- and we will look at

- but wind

- or wind

Create: _____

_____

_____

4. Start: However, the moon does have mountains _____.

    Add: One of the following, using a phrase that makes sense.

- or valleys

- and valleys

- but valleys

Create: _____

_____

_____

(**PART A**) *Sharpening Your Word Choices*

Everyone wants to ~~help~~ the panda. It is one of the world's

most popular animals and one of the most endangered. The

government of China is doing everything it can to ~~help~~ the panda.

The World Wildlife Federation (WWF) is ~~helping~~ the Chinese

government. In addition, the WWF is asking you to ~~help~~. You

can go to the WWF Web site to learn ways you can ~~help~~.

PART B *Polishing Your Sentences (Sentence Combining)*

Topic Sentence: Honeybees are very social insects.

1. Start: Bees not only live together _____ .

     Add: One of the following, using a phrase that makes sense.

- but also work together

- or also work together

- but also have a head, thorax, and abdomen

Create: _____

_____

_____

2. Start: Almost all bees search for nectar and pollen _____.

     Add: One of the following, using a clause that makes sense.

- and the queen does other things

- or the queen does other things

- but the queen does other things

Create: _____

_____

_____

3. Start: The queen bee is in charge of the hive _____.

   Add: One of the following, using a phrase that makes sense.

   • and produces all the offspring

   • but produces all the offspring

   • or produces all the offspring

Create: _____

_____

_____

PART A *Sharpening Your Word Choices*

All around the world, humans ~~build~~ treehouses. Adults often ~~build~~ treehouses for everyday living or for leisure. On the other hand, children usually ~~build~~ treehouses as hideaways. These treehouses are secret places full of adventure, for sleeping outside, for storing treasures, or for finding peace away from the busy world. Or, maybe someone builds a treehouse just for a way to be up high and live like the birds.

PART B *Polishing Your Sentences (Sentence Combining)*

Topic Sentence: In ancient Greece, one of the most important city–states was Athens.

1. Start: Athens, Greece, was known for its beautiful buildings, _____ .

Add: Three of the following, using parallel structure.

- and life-like statues
- and went to war with Sparta
- and development of theater
- and democratic government
- and wore tunics

Create: _____

_____

_____

_____

2. Start: A queen _____ did not rule Athens.

Add: One of following, using a phrase that makes sense.

- but king
- or king
- but known for its citizens

Create: _____

_____

3. Start: Instead, citizens voted on important issues such as whether to go to war _____.

Add: One of the following, using a phrase that makes sense.

- or negotiate for peace

- but negotiate for peace

- and decided things for the community

Create: _____

_____

_____

_____

50

My friend Stacey likes to ~~think~~ about taking "The Rocky Mountaineer" train through the breathtaking scenery of Canada. People ~~think~~ of this trip as "the most spectacular train trip in the world." The train travels through miles and miles of snow-capped mountains. Stacey ~~thinks~~ that this adventure would be valuable for her, giving her time away from her busy life to relax and ~~think~~.

PART B *Editing Your Paragraph*

Sound good?
Combine?
Omit?
Replace?
Expand?

a. As you read the paragraph aloud, ask yourself, "Does it **sound good**?"

b. **Combine** sentences 1 and 2.

c. **Omit** an unnecessary word in sentence 4. (Make an X.)

d. **Combine** sentences 3 and 4.

e. **Combine** sentences 5 and 6.

f. **Combine** sentences 8 and 9.

g. **Replace** the underlined word in sentence 8 with a new word choice.

h. **Combine** sentences 10 and 11.

¹Each class had its picture taken. ²This happened on the last day of school. ³The teachers lined up. ⁴All members of the our class lined up. ⁵Some of us sat on benches. ⁶Others stood in the back. ⁷We laughed and giggled and made faces. ⁸The <u>nice</u> photographer tried to be serious. ⁹He kept cracking up. ¹⁰We couldn't wait for school to end. ¹¹We couldn't wait for vacation to begin.

Edited paragraph:

_____

_____

_____

_____

_____

_____

_____

_____

_____

_____

PART A *Sharpening Your Word Choices*

The fire at the Village Green Apartments was a very sad event for the Habib family. Each member of the family lost something in the blaze. Mrs. Habib was ~~sad~~ over the loss of the family photographs. Mr. Habib was ~~sad~~ at losing a collection of rare books. Kareem and Sarah were ~~sad~~ that some of their favorite clothes suffered severe smoke damage. Young Elish was the ~~saddest~~ of all because his pet gerbils died in the fire.

PART B *Polishing Your Sentences (Sentence Combining)*

Topic Sentence: Mark, the adventurer, is on his way to observe
the baboons in Africa.

1. Start: Baboons fascinate him.

Add: They act so much like humans. (When the second idea
tells *why*, use *because* to make one sentence.)

Create: _____

_____

_____

2. Start: Baboons seem so much like humans.

Add: Their anatomies are so similar. (When the second idea
tells *why*, use *because* to make one sentence.)

Create: _____

_____

_____

3. Start: A baboon looks like it is deep in thought.

Add: It looks like it is deep in thought *when* it raises its clenched hand up to its chin.

Create: _____

_____

_____

_____

_____

4. Start: Baboons are now considered as smart as apes or chimpanzees.

Add: Scientists have found evidence of abstract thought in baboons. (When the second idea tells *why*, use *because* to make one sentence.)

Create: _____

_____

_____

_____

_____

_____

Many tourists in England and the United States visit toy museums while on vacation. The World's Largest Toy Museum is in Branson, Missouri, in the United States. It has a large collection of ~~old~~ trains, boats, dolls, and cap guns. Pollock's Toy Museum in London, England, has many ~~old~~ mechanical toys. The Toy Town Museum in East Aurora, New York, displays a large collection of ~~old~~ wooden pull-toys.

PART B *Polishing Your Sentences (Sentence Combining)*

Topic Sentence: Mark, the adventurer, is about to see the newly discovered colossal squid, which is seven feet longer than the giant squid.

1. Start: Mark will be visiting New Zealand's national museum.

Add: He can see this wondrous discovery with his own eyes. (When the second idea tells *why*, use *so* to make one sentence.)

Create: _____

_____

_____

2. Start: The colossal squid has up to 25 teeth-like swiveling hooks at the ends of its arms and tentacles.

Add: It can defend itself against hungry sperm whales. (When the second idea tells *why*, use *so* to make one sentence.)

Create: _____

_____

_____

3. Start: The colossal squid has two large parrot-like beaks.

    Add: The colossal squid has two eyes the size of dinner plates.

    Create: _____

_____

_____

_____

4. Start: The squid's body glows in the dark.

    Add: The massive eyes can use the light to see its prey. (When the second idea tells _why_, use _so_ to make one sentence.)

    Create: _____

_____

_____

_____

(**PART A**) *Sharpening Your Word Choices*

Cleanliness is very important in the food service industry.

Restaurant owners must keep their kitchens ~~clean~~ to prevent

the spread of disease. Countertops and cutting boards must be

~~clean~~. Towels and sponges must be clean to prevent the growth

of bacteria. Cleanliness is also important for safety. ~~Clean~~ floors

prevent kitchen workers from slipping and injuring themselves.

Finally, cleanliness keeps customers coming back. Few customers

enjoy a "greasy spoon."

(**PART B**) *Polishing Your Sentences (Sentence Combining)*

Topic Sentence: While he is in New Zealand, Mark, the adventurer,
is studying yellow-eyed penguins.

1. Start: He is learning about yellow-eyed penguins.

   Add: He is making a TV show about them. (When the second idea tells
why, use *to* to make one sentence.)

   Create: _____

   _____

   _____

2. Start: He agreed to make the TV show.

   Add: He is dispelling the popular myth that all penguins
live on ice floes. (When the second idea tells *why*,
use *to* to make one sentence.)

   Create: _____

   _____

   _____

   _____

   _____

   _____

3. Start: Yellow-eyed penguins have lived for thousands of years.

    Add: They have lived in forests.

    Add: The forests are near the coast of New Zealand.

    Create: _____

_____

_____

4. Start: The penguins take daily trips to the ocean.

    Add: They are searching for sprat.

    Add: They are searching for red cod.

    Add: They are searching for small squid. (When the second idea tells *why*, use *to* to make one sentence.)

    Create: _____

_____

_____

PART A *Sharpening Your Word Choices*

Actors often enjoy playing the role of the villain. Nothing is

quite as fun as being the ~~mean~~ character in a play. Wouldn't you

have fun being a ~~mean~~ neighbor or a ~~mean~~ landlord? Wouldn't

it be fun to have theater-goers booing at you as you play the role

of a ~~mean~~ criminal or a ~~mean~~ thug? Acting lets you pretend to

be someone you would not choose to be in real life.

PART B *Polishing Your Sentences (Sentence Combining)*

Topic Sentence: Mark, the adventurer, is leaving New Zealand and stopping off in Australia to photograph the duck-billed platypus.

1. Start: The platypus is a special kind of mammal called a monotreme.

Add: The platypus lays eggs. (When the second idea tells *why*, use *to*, *so that*, or *because* to make one sentence.)

Create: _____

_____

_____

_____

2. Start: The word monotreme is rarely heard.

Add: Only two animals belong to this subfamily of mammals. (When the second idea tells *why*, use *to*, *so that*, or *because* to make one sentence.)

Create: _____

_____

_____

_____

_____

3. Start: The platypus injects venom into its enemies with a sharp, horny spur on its hind leg.

    Add: The platypus protects itself against predators. (When the second idea tells why, use *to*, *so that*, or *because* to make one sentence.)

Create: _____

_____

_____

_____

_____

_____

PART A *Sharpening Your Word Choices*

Learning a new language can be a ~~hard~~ task for some people

and an exciting challenge for others. Memorizing thousands

of new words is ~~hard~~, of course, but it is also ~~hard~~ to learn a

new way of putting words together into sentences. Speaking

in a different language can be a ~~hard~~ activity, particularly if

you continue to think in your native language instead of trying

to think in the new language.

PART B   *Editing Your Paragraph*

Sound good?
Combine?
Omit?
Replace?
Expand?

a.   As you read the paragraph aloud, ask yourself, "Does it **sound good**?"

b.   **Combine** sentences 1 and 2. (Remember, when the second idea tells *why*, use the words **to**, **so that**, or **because** to make one sentence.)

c.   **Expand** sentence 3. Add your own word or words that describe what kind of digger the aardvark is.

d.   **Omit** an unnecessary word in sentence 4. (Make an X.)

e.   Does sentence 5 **sound good**? If not, correct the errors.

f.   **Combine** sentences 5 and 6.

g.   **Combine** sentences 8 and 9.

¹After Mark, the adventurer, leaves Australia, he heads for Africa. ²He learns more about the talented aardvark. ³The aardvark is a digger. ⁴It can dig scoop out a four-foot-long tunnel faster than six men with shovels! ⁵The aardvark does a lot of dig. ⁶It can find enough insects for its dinner. ⁷It doesn't have to go far to begin finding them. ⁸The insects are attracted to the aardvark. ⁹It smells like rotten fruit.

Edited paragraph:

_____

_____

_____

_____

_____

_____

_____

_____

_____

_____

_____

_____

PART A *Sharpening Your Word Choices*

Marcus raced _____ to shop class, but Jason shuffled
(see *ran*)   (see *walked*)

_____ down the hall. Both boys knew that their birdhouse

projects were due today. Marcus had toiled _____ all
(see *worked*)

semester to create a sturdy yet exquisite birdhouse. Jason,

on the other hand, had worked _____, resulting in a

birdhouse that could barely stand up. As they took their seats,

Marcus whispered _____ to Jason, "I think we can fix
(see *talked*)

your birdhouse if we both work _____. Do you want

some help?"

PART B *Polishing Your Sentences (Sentence Combining)*

Topic Sentence: Marcus and Jason met to work on Jason's birdhouse.

1. Start: They thought about the materials they would need.

Add: They were like two generals plotting an attack.

Create: _____

_____

_____

_____

2. Start: They cut the wood.

Add: They cut it with precision.

Add: They were like two surgeons during a delicate operation.

Create: _____

_____

_____

3. Start: They nailed the sides together.

Add: They fastened the roof to the sides.

Add: They fastened it securely.

Create: _____

_____

_____

4. Start: They sanded its sides and corners.

Add: They sanded gently.

Add: They painted it blue.

Add: They sanded and painted after lunch.

Create: _____

_____

_____

PART A *Sharpening Your Word Choices*

Opening night of the musical was far from perfect. The

talented soloists sang _____, but behind the scenes

they argued _____ over missed cues. While the lead

performers acted _____, the supporting cast performed
(see *acted*)

_____, constantly stealing each other's lines. The children's

choir sang _____ but was difficult to hear. Despite

the dismal performance, the audience _____

gave the cast a round of applause.

PART B *Polishing Your Sentences (Sentence Combining)*

Topic Sentence: Mr. Jefferson, the choir director, was very disappointed in the choir's performance.

1. Start: He decided to improve their singing.

Add: He would require them to come to extra rehearsals. (When the second idea tells *how*, use *by* to make one sentence.)

Create: _____

_____

_____

2. Start: He stopped bad behavior.

Add: The behavior was during class.

Add: He assigned everyone to new seats. (When the second idea tells *how*, use *by* to make one sentence.)

Create: _____

_____

_____

_____

3. Start: He knew the singers would improve.

Add: They would practice vocal exercises.

Add: The exercises are difficult. (When the second idea tells *how*, use *by* to make one sentence.)

Create: _____

_____

_____

4. Start: The choir sang.

Add: They sang harmoniously.

Add: They did this after several weeks of practice.

Create: _____

_____

_____

_____

PART A   *Sharpening Your Word Choices*

The two candidates stepped onto the stage for the political

debate. First, the moderator introduced Martha Ryan, a

widely respected public servant who had conducted herself

(see behaved)

_____ and _____ in her last elected position.

Martha spoke _____ and _____ as she shared

her vision for the city. Next, the moderator introduced Amie

Franklin, a politician despised by many in the audience. Amie

spoke _____, showing disdain for the audience and

her opponent. Most people agreed that she behaved _____

during the debate.

PART B   *Polishing Your Sentences (Sentence Combining)*

Topic Sentence: No one knows how Amie Franklin was ever
elected to office.

1. Start: She made many voters mad.

   Add: The voters were in her district.

   Add: She ignored their letters. (When the second idea
tells *how*, use *by* to make one sentence.)

   Create: _____

   _____

   _____

2. Start: She ruined most conversations.

   Add: She ranted about other politicians. (When the
second idea tells *how*, use *by* to make one sentence.)

   Create: _____

   _____

   _____

3. Start: She barked at her opponent.

Add: She barked like a dog frightened by its shadow.

Add: She did this during debates.

Create: _____

_____

_____

4. Start: She won her first election.

Add: She spent amounts of money.

Add: The amounts were huge. (When the second
idea tells *how*, use *by* to make one sentence.)

Create: _____

_____

_____

Beverly Cleary is a famous writer of children's stories. When

she was a child, she longed to read funny stories about the sort

of children she knew. As an adult, she wrote _____

about a girl named Ramona Quimby. Mrs. Cleary had no

trouble writing _____ about Ramona. You see,
      (see *wrote*)

Mrs. Cleary was really telling about herself when she was a

young girl. After telling about many of Ramona's adventures,

Mrs. Cleary switched to writing about a boy named Leigh

Botts. Some readers were disappointed, but many cheered

_____ for her new character. Around the world,

children respond _____ when they receive one of
         (see *responded*)

Mrs. Cleary's books.

PART B *Polishing Your Sentences (Sentence Combining)*

Topic Sentence: Ramona was one of Beverly Cleary's favorite characters.

1. Start: Ramona was mischievous.

Add: She could also be lovable. (Use *but* to make one sentence.)

Create: _____

_____

_____

2. Start: As a four-year-old, she got into trouble.

Add: She teased her friends. (When the second idea tells *how*, use *by* to make one sentence.)

Add: She was a pest. (Also tells *how* she got into trouble.)

Create: _____

_____

_____

3. Start: In fourth grade, she became friends with Daisy.

Add: She shared her corn chips.

Add: She shared them at lunch. (When the second idea tells *how*, use *by* to make one sentence.)

Create: _____

_____

_____

_____

4. Start: She was always early to school.

Add: She didn't want to miss anything that might happen. (When the second idea tells *why*, use *to*, *so that*, or *because* to make one sentence.)

Create: _____

_____

_____

_____

_____

60

After winning three gold medals in the 1960 Olympics,

Wilma Rudolph was called "the fastest woman in the world."

However, it is the story of her early life that made her a legend.

Wilma had many childhood diseases, including polio, which left

her without the use of her left leg. Fitted with metal leg braces,

she moved _____ and _____. Fortunately, she

responded _____ to treatment and, through determination,
(see *answered*)

was out of her braces by age nine. Wilma began running in

track meets even before she went to college. As a natural

runner, she moved _____ and _____. Later, as a coach,

she _____ shared what she had learned with her

runners, urging them to have confidence in themselves.

PART B *Editing Your Paragraph*

Sound good?
Combine?
Omit?
Replace?
Expand?

a. As you read the paragraph aloud, ask yourself, "Does it **sound good**?"
b. **Combine** sentences 1 and 2.
c. **Combine** sentences 3 and 4.
d. **Combine** sentences 5, 6, and 7.
e. **Omit** an unnecessary word in sentence 8. (Make an X.)
f. **Replace** the underlined word in sentence 10 with a more interesting word.
g. **Combine** sentences 8, 9, and 10.
h. **Expand** by adding a word or phrase in sentence 11 that tells *how* researchers have worked.

¹Acute polio lasts less than two weeks. ²Its damage to the human nervous system could last a lifetime. ³About 20–40% of polio survivors develop post-polio syndrome (PPS). ⁴They develop it later in life. ⁵Polio survivors can overcome their weakness. ⁶They exercise. ⁷They get plenty of rest. ⁸Some people with PPS must also take medication, too. ⁹They take it to lessen the pain. ¹⁰They take it to <u>help</u> their breathing. ¹¹Researchers have worked to find effective treatments for those with PPS.

Edited paragraph:

_____

_____

_____

_____

_____

_____

_____

_____

_____

_____

_____

_____

> **Directions:** In the paragraph below, find eight cases where the subject and verb do not match. Correct the errors.

It is a beautiful spring day. Children ~~is~~ playing baseball. Matt sits on the edge of the outfield and ~~wish~~ that he could join them. However, he is new at the school and ~~are~~ very shy. He played baseball almost every day in his old hometown and misses the fun of competition. As he watches, a ball ~~sail~~ high up in the air towards him. Without thinking, Matt ~~stand~~ up, ~~lift~~ up his arm, and makes the perfect catch. Matt's face turns red as he ~~wonder~~, "Will they be mad at me?" Then he ~~see~~ Jake, the team captain, walking toward him with a huge smile.

(PART B) *Polishing Your Sentences (Sentence Combining)*

Topic Sentence: Dennis and Mick discovered the basement was a real mess.

1. Start: Mick ran upstairs to get cleaning supplies.

Add: Dennis made a list of things to do. (Use *while* or *when* to make one sentence.)

Create: _____

_____

_____

2. Start: Mick came back downstairs.

Add: Dennis and Mick divided up the cleaning tasks. (Use *while* or *when* to make one sentence.)

Create: _____

_____

_____

_____

3. Start: Mick organized the boxes.

Add: Dennis swept the floor. (Use *while* or *when* to make one sentence.)

Create: _____

_____

_____

_____

4. Start: Mick locked up.

Add: Dennis thought about tomorrow's tasks.

Add: This happened at the end of the day. (Use *while* or *when* to make one sentence.)

Create: _____

_____

_____

_____

PART A *Sharpening Your Word Choices*

Directions: In the paragraph below, find four cases where the subject and verb do not match. Correct the errors.

This summer we ~~is~~ having a BIG family reunion. My mother and father are coming to the mountain retreat. Unfortunately, my sister, her husband, and three of their children are unable to join us. However, Peter, their oldest son, ~~are~~ planning on being there. Uncles, aunts, and 23 cousins ~~is~~ definitely attending, which will make the event exciting. We have scheduled many activities. The picnic, the sing-along, and the game night ~~is~~ always the favorites.

PART B *Polishing Your Sentences (Sentence Combining)*

Topic Sentence: Teresa is exhausted.

1. Start: She had been counting sheep.

Add: She went to bed.

Add: She did this at 8:00 a.m.
(Use *since* to make one sentence.)

Create: _____

_____

_____

2. Start: She hasn't been getting much sleep.

Add: She started working nights.
(Use *since* to make one sentence.)

Create: _____

_____

_____

_____

3. Start: She has had to sleep during the day.

Add: Dogs and children play outside.

Add: They play noisily. (Use *while* or *when* to make one sentence.)

Create: _____

_____

_____

4. Start: Her alarm went off at 2 p.m.

Add: She felt like she hadn't slept at all.
(Use *while* or *when* to make one sentence.)

Create: _____

_____

_____

> **Directions:** In the paragraph below, find three cases where the subject and verb do not agree. Correct the errors.

We are not certain of our vacation plans. Either the whole family or just the boys ~~is~~ going on a trip. Neither my mother nor father ~~are~~ interested in going to Disneyland, so we will probably go camping. Neither my older brother nor two younger brothers ~~is~~ fans of camping, but they will make the best of it. Our next-door neighbors or one of our cousins is always included in our plans.

DETOUR

p. 221

PART B *Polishing Your Sentences (Sentence Combining)*

Topic Sentence: The Porcupine caribou herd is the largest herd
in the Arctic Refuge (ANWR).

1. Start: Porcupine caribou are large mammals.

   Add: Porcupine caribou are hoofed mammals.

   Add: They live in northern Canada.

   Add: They live in eastern Alaska.
   (Use *that* to make one sentence.)

Create: _____

_____

_____

_____

2. Start: They follow a migration route.

   Add: The route can take them over 3,000 miles (4,875 km) of terrain.

   Add: They do this each year.
   (Use *that* to make one sentence.)

Create: _____

_____

_____

_____

3. Start: Porcupine caribou look for habitats.

Add: They do this during their travels.

Add: The habitats provide them with food, water, and protection from predators.
(Use *that* to make one sentence.)

Create: _____

_____

_____

_____

4. Start: They find lichen, moss, and small shrubs to eat.

Add: They dig holes in the snow.

Add: They do this in the winter.
(Use *by* to make one sentence.)

Create: _____

_____

_____

PART A *Sharpening Your Word Choices*

Help Book
85

> **Directions:** In the paragraph below, find three cases where the subject and verb do not agree. Correct the errors.

Don is remodeling a house that he hopes to sell for a profit. Luckily, neither the windows nor the front door ~~need~~ to be replaced. Those would be expensive projects. Likewise, neither the back door nor the screens ~~needs~~ replacement. The kitchen needs to be updated, but at least it has no plumbing problems. On the other hand, the floors, the molding, and the railings all require repairs. Either the carpenters or Don ~~are~~ going to do the work. They will decide next week.

PART B *Polishing Your Sentences (Sentence Combining)*

Topic Sentence: Teenagers looking for work with the public should consider their appearance.

1. Start: (Some) teens wish to be employed at restaurants.

Add: They must heed this advice.

Create: _____

_____

_____

2. Start: (Some) restaurants hire young workers.

Add: They want employees who look responsible.

Create: _____

_____

_____

3. Start: (Some) shirts are unbuttoned or not tucked in.

Add: They do not make a good impression.

Create: _____

_____

_____

4. Start: (Some) pants are too baggy.

Add: (Some) pants are too long.

Add: They do not look professional.

Create: _____

_____

_____

(**PART A**) *Sharpening Your Word Choices*

Directions: In the paragraph below, find three cases where the subject and verb do not agree. Correct the errors.

That woman with the small poodles lives in my neighborhood.

Her poodles, Elsie and Max, ~~is~~ very lively. Their mother, a toy

poodle, and their father, a miniature poodle, ~~is~~ often seen at dog

shows. Unfortunately, neither Elsie nor Max ~~are~~ well-mannered

enough to be entered into a dog show, even if they were eligible.

My neighbor, who adores her puppies, is not upset by their

unruly behavior.

PART B *Editing Your Paragraph*

Sound good?
Combine?
Omit?
Replace?
Expand?

a. As you read the paragraph aloud, ask yourself, "Does it **sound good?**"

b. **Combine** sentences 1, 2, and 3. Does the sentence **sound good?** (Do the subject and verb agree? If not, correct the error.)

c. **Omit** an unnecessary word in sentence 4. (Make an X.)

d. Does sentence 5 **sound good?** Do the subject and verb agree? If not, correct the error.

e. **Replace** the underlined words in sentence 5 with two new words.

f. **Combine** sentences 6 and 7.

g. **Expand** sentence 7. Add words that tell *why* the small dogs move their legs as fast as they can.

h. Does sentence 8 **sound good?** Do the subject and verb agree? If not, correct the error.

¹Pamela walks down my street. ²Her three dogs walks down my street. ³This happens every day. ⁴The dogs take and their owner take the same walk every day at the same time. ⁵The <u>big</u> dog with <u>big</u> feet pull hard on his leash. ⁶The other two dogs, who are much smaller, move their legs. ⁷They move them as fast as they can. ⁸I wonder whether the dogs or Pamela get the most exercise from their walk.

Edited paragraph:

_____

_____

_____

_____

_____

_____

_____

_____

_____

_____

66

Help Book
87

PART A   *Sharpening Your Word Choices*

Directions: In the paragraph below, find three cases where the subject and verb do not agree. Correct the errors.

"OH NO! School pictures are today and I FORGOT.

Either my teacher or my mother ~~are~~ responsible for this

disaster. Neither my clothes nor my hair ~~are~~ right for pictures.

The hole in my pants ~~look~~ ugly. My blouse is stained. And worst

of all, I wore socks of two different colors! Maybe I could hide

for a few days in the coat closet."

PART B *Polishing Your Sentences (Sentence Combining)*

Topic Sentence: As we do every year, my friends and I watched the Academy Awards on TV.

1. Start: The award for best supporting actor went to a man.

Add: The man played a clever thief.

Create: _____

_____

_____

2. Start: The Academy presented a special award to a woman.

Add: The woman had done excellent work.

Add: She had done it throughout her whole career.

Create: _____

_____

_____

3. Start: The Oscar for best actor was awarded to a young actor.

Add: The actor wasn't well known.

Create: _____

_____

_____

4. Start: The Oscar for best director was given to a woman.

Add: The woman had made several fine films.

Add: The woman had never won an award.
(Combine these sentences using *who* and *but*.)

Create: _____

_____

_____

> **Directions:** In the paragraph below, find four cases where the subject and verb do not agree. Correct the errors.

Eva Granger, the president of the Evergreen Nursery, oversees the 14 employees and all company operations. Each of the employees ~~make~~ a unique contribution to the company. Several ~~is~~ managers of specific departments: garden plants, trees, garden equipment, and lawn treatments. Others work under the direction of the managers. Everybody ~~are~~ required to give quality service. Everyone ~~try~~ to listen to the customers and politely answer their questions.

(PART B) *Polishing Your Sentences (Sentence Combining)*

Topic Sentence: Watching what you eat is the key to improving your health.

1. Start: (Some) people have high blood pressure.

Add: They should reduce fat in their diet.

Add: They should reduce sodium in their diet.

Create: _____

_____

_____

2. Start: Someone is anemic.

Add: He should eat lots of fish.

Add: He should eat lots of liver.

Add: He should eat lots of green leafy vegetables.

Create: _____

_____

_____

3. Start: (Some) people have calcium deficiencies.

     Add: They should eat foods such as milk and cheese.

     Add: These foods are calcium-rich.

     Create: _____

_____

_____

_____

4. Start: (Some) foods are good for the heart.

     Add: These foods are low in fat.

     Create: _____

_____

_____

PART A *Sharpening Your Word Choices*

> **Directions:** In the paragraph below, find four cases where the subject and verb do not agree. Correct the errors.

Everyone ~~believe~~ that recycling is needed so that natural resources will not be used up. Everybody ~~know~~ that we should recycle materials such as paper and cans, reuse items such as glass jars and paper bags, and reduce the use of Styrofoam and plastics. However, many people do not participate in recycling while others ~~is~~ very inconsistent. Anyone who is diligent at recycling ~~are~~ performing a service for all of us.

PART B *Polishing Your Sentences (Sentence Combining)*

Topic Sentence: I've given up on the Eagles, our football team.

1. Start: Will they win or lose?

Add: It is not important to me.
(Combine these sentences by using *whether*.)

Create: _____

_____

_____

2. Start: They did something on the field.

Add: It embarrassed their fans.
(Combine these sentences by using *what*.)

Create: _____

_____

_____

3. Start: They chose to run.

Add: They did this in the last play.

Add: It is a mystery to me.
(Combine these sentences by using *why*.)

Create: _____

_____

_____

4. Start: I will do something now.

Add: I will watch basketball or soccer instead.
(Combine these sentences by using *whether*, *why*, or *what*.)

Create: _____

_____

_____

PART A   *Sharpening Your Word Choices*

> **Directions:** In the paragraph below, find four cases where the subject and verb do not agree. Correct the errors.

Jason wanted to join the water polo team for many reasons. Here ~~are~~ his thinking. Neither his three older brothers nor his younger brother ~~have~~ ever been on a water polo team. Several brothers ~~has~~ played football. Everyone has turned out for track, although they excelled in different events. But, there ~~is~~ no water polo players in the family. Water polo would be all HIS.

PART B   *Polishing Your Sentences (Sentence Combining)*

Topic Sentence: Mysteries are fun to read.

1. Start: What is going to happen next?

     Add: The reader seldom knows.
             (Combine these sentences with *who*, *what*, or *that*.)

     Create: _____

_____

_____

2. Start: Who committed the crime?

   Add: You might be able to guess.

   Add: You might do it before the last chapter.
   (Combine these sentences with *who*, *what*, or *that*.)

   Create: _____

   _____

   _____

3. Start: What happens in the story?

   Add: You have to follow very carefully.
   (Combine these sentences with *who*, *what*, or *that*.)

   Create: _____

   _____

   _____

4. Start: The butler did it.

   Add: Some people always think this.
   (Combine these sentences with *who*, *what*, or *that*.)

   Create: _____

   _____

   _____

(**PART A**)   *Sharpening Your Word Choices*

Directions: In the paragraph below, find six cases where the
subject and verb do not agree. Correct the errors.

The jury has been deliberating for five days. Here ~~are~~ the

reason. The evidence concerning the robbery was very confusing.

The victim's family ~~have~~ argued that the defendant ~~were~~ walking

in their neighborhood on the evening of the crime. However,

his basketball team ~~were~~ insisting that he was across town at a

practice. There ~~were~~ also a question about the stolen item. No

one could figure out if the bicycle belonged to the victim or the

defendant. The jury ~~are~~ permanently deadlocked.

PART B) *Editing Your Paragraph*

Sound good?
Combine?
Omit?
Replace?
Expand?

a. As you read the paragraph aloud, ask yourself, "Does it **sound good?**"

b. Does sentence 1 **sound good?** If not, correct it.

c. **Expand** sentence 2. Add words that tell *where*.

d. Does sentence 3 **sound good?** If not, correct it.

e. **Combine** sentences 3 and 4.

f. Does sentence 5 **sound good?** If not, correct it.

g. Does sentence 6 **sound good?** If not, correct it.

h. **Replace** the underlined word in sentence 6 with a more interesting word.

i. **Replace** the underlined word in sentence 7 with a more interesting word.

j. **Combine** sentences 8 and 9 using **or**. Does the new sentence **sound good?** If not, correct it.

¹When most people in the Northern Hemisphere thinks about baseball, they think about summer, but in Puerto Rico, winter is the baseball season. ²Baseball is one of the most popular sports.

³People on this Caribbean island crowds the ballparks to see major league teams compete. ⁴They do this every winter. ⁵The game tickets costs one tenth of what they would cost in the States.

⁶Everybody get <u>good</u> snacks, great seats, and players' autographs.

[7]The players are quite <u>good</u>. [8]There is many players who have

been given scholarships to U.S. colleges. [9]There is many who have

signed contracts with pro teams.

Edited paragraph:

_____

_____

_____

_____

_____

_____

_____

_____

_____

_____

Directions: In the paragraph below, at least ten possibilities exist for making changes. Your task is to make at least seven changes. This includes finding four cases where the subject and verb do not agree.

In the trees near Eugene, Oregon, live a surprising resident, a big, gray female coyote named Silver. While most coyotes lives in remote places, Silver and a group of six other coyotes has created a good life in a big residential area of town. With the increasing destruction of their wilderness habitat, more and more coyotes is living in populated places.

PART B *Editing Your Paragraph*

Sound good?
Combine?
Omit?
Replace?
Expand?

a. As you read the paragraph aloud, ask yourself, "Does it **sound good**?"

b. **Combine** sentences 3, 4, and 5.

c. Does sentence 6 **sound good**? If not, correct it.

d. Does sentence 7 **sound good**? If not, correct it.

e. **Combine** sentences 8 and 9. (Hint: Use **when**.)

f. **Combine** sentences 10 and 11. (Hint: Begin the new sentence with **Because**.)

g. **Expand** sentence 12 by adding a phrase that tells *where*. (Hint: Use the information in sentence 11 to help you.)

¹Water moving from the Earth's surface into the atmosphere and back again is called the water cycle. ²The Earth would not have its weather without this water cycle. ³The water cycle consists of evaporation. ⁴It also consists of condensation. ⁵It also consists of precipitation. ⁶Evaporation are the process of a liquid turning into a gas. ⁷In the Earth's water cycle, the heat of the sun cause water to evaporate. ⁸Water becomes water vapor. ⁹The water evaporates. ¹⁰The water vapor is warm. ¹¹The water vapor rises into the upper atmosphere. ¹²The temperature is cooler.

Edited paragraph:

_____

_____

_____

_____

_____

_____

_____

_____

_____

_____

_____

_____

_____

_____

_____

PART A *Sharpening Your Word Choices*

Directions: In the paragraph below, at least ten possibilities exist for making changes. Your task is to make at least five changes. This includes finding two cases where the subject and verb do not agree.

Silver and her group walk over a big place, hunting for food day and night. While these coyotes still eat their usual fare of rabbits, mice, ground squirrels, and insects, they likes finding urban food such as garbage, dog food, and little domestic animals. Of course, coming into someone's yard to snatch food doesn't make a favorable impression on humans. In fact, many people believe these coyotes is bad and mean.

PART B *Editing Your Paragraph*

a.   As you read the paragraph aloud, ask yourself, "Does it **sound good?**"

b.   **Combine** sentences 1 and 2. (Hint: Combine these sentences by using **and**.)

c.   Does sentence 3 **sound good**? If not, correct it.

d.   **Combine** sentences 3 and 4.

e.   **Combine** sentences 5 and 6.

f.   **Combine** sentences 7 and 8.

g.   **Combine** sentences 9 and 10. (Hint: Combine these sentences by using **when** and by using a **comma**.)

h.   **Combine** sentences 11 and 12.

i.   **Combine** sentences 14 and 15. (Hint: Combine these sentences by using **that**.)

¹In the last lesson, you learned about the water cycle. ²You learned about the relationship of the water cycle to the Earth's weather. ³When we left off, water vapor were rising. ⁴It was rising into the cooler atmosphere. ⁵In the cold atmosphere, the water vapor cools, and condensation occurs. ⁶The water vapor was warm. ⁷Condensation is the process of a gas turning into a liquid. ⁸It is also the process of a gas turning into a solid. ⁹Water

vapor condenses. [10]It becomes microscopic drops of water. [11]The water gathers around dust particles. [12]It forms clouds. [13]As more and more water gathers around the dust, the clouds get heavier and heavier. [14]Sometimes, the temperature in the clouds is cold enough. [15]The water turns into ice.

72

Edited paragraph:

_____

_____

_____

_____

_____

_____

_____

_____

_____

_____

_____

_____

_____

_____

_____

_____

_____

PART A *Sharpening Your Word Choices*

> **Directions:** In the paragraph below, more than ten possibilities exist for making changes. Your task is to make at least ten changes. This includes finding six cases where the subject and verb do not agree.

Once a year, Silver make a den in preparation for having a group of three to nine pups. When the little pups is first born, they is blind and helpless. For three months, they stay in the den while Silver and her mate hunts for food. When the little pups grow, they ~~is~~ taught how to hunt. After only one year, the pups know how to take care of themselves and is soon going in the neighborhoods of Eugene.

(PART B) *Editing Your Paragraph*

Sound good?
Combine?
Omit?
Replace?
Expand?

a. As you read the paragraph aloud, ask yourself, "Does it **sound good**?"

b. **Combine** sentences 2 and 3. (Hint: Combine these sentences by using **when** and by using a **comma**.)

c. **Combine** sentences 4 and 5. (Hint: Combine with **to**.)

d. Does sentence 6 **sound good**? If not, correct it.

e. **Combine** sentences 7 and 8. (Hint: Begin the new sentence with **When**.)

f. Does sentence 9 **sound good**? If not, correct it.

g. **Combine** sentences 10 and 11. (Hint: Combine these sentences by using **and** and by using **commas**.)

h. **Combine** sentences 12, 13, 14, 15, and 16. (Hint: Combine these sentences by using **to**, by using **commas**, and by using **or**.)

¹Let's review part of what you learned in the last lesson.

²The water vapor is high in the cold atmosphere. ³The water

vapor condenses into water and sometimes ice. ⁴The water

and ice gather around dust particles. ⁵Gathering around dust

particles forms clouds. ⁶The clouds becomes heavier and heavier.

⁷The clouds become too heavy. ⁸The water or ice falls to the

Earth. ⁹The process of water or ice falling to the Earth are called precipitation. [10]Rain and sleet are types of precipitation. [11]Hail and snow are types of precipitation. [12]Look out the window.

[13]Look out the window now. [14]You are seeing if evaporation is happening. [15]You are seeing if condensation is happening.

[16]You are seeing if precipitation is happening.

Edited paragraph:

_____

_____

_____

_____

_____

_____

_____

_____

_____

_____

_____

_____

_____

_____

_____

_____

PART A   *Sharpening Your Word Choices*

Directions: In the paragraph below, more than ten possibilities exist for making changes. Your task is to make at least six changes. This includes finding three cases where the subject and verb do not agree.

Silver have all the coyote traits that make catching prey fairly easy. First, she have a good sense of hearing that lets her find prey and avoid danger. Second, her sense of smell helps her find not only her prey but also the territories of other coyotes, which are marked by their scent. In addition, Silver can ran 25 to 30 miles per hour, making it hard for her prey to escape. Finally, Silver are very smart, so her prey cannot outsmart her.

(**PART B**) *Editing Your Paragraph*

Sound good?
Combine?
Omit?
Replace?
Expand?

a. As you read the paragraph aloud, ask yourself, "Does it **sound good**?"

b. **Combine** sentences 1, 2, and 3.

c. Does sentence 4 **sound good**? If not, correct it.

d. **Combine** sentences 4, 5, and 6. (Hint: Combine these sentences by using **and**.)

e. Does sentence 7 **sound good**? If not, correct it.

f. **Combine** sentences 9 and 10. (Hint: Combine these sentences by using **and**.)

g. Does sentence 11 **sound good**? If not, correct it.

h. **Combine** sentences 11 and 12. (Hint: Begin the new sentence with **As**.)

i. **Combine** sentences 13, 14, 15, and 16. (Hint: Begin the new sentence with **When** and combine these sentences by using **or** and by using **and**.)

¹In the last three lessons, you learned about evaporation. ²You learned about condensation. ³You learned about precipitation. ⁴The sun's heat evaporate water. ⁵The warm water vapor rises high into the atmosphere. ⁶The atmosphere is cold. ⁷The cold atmosphere cause the warm water vapor to condense into very small drops of water or ice. ⁸The water and ice gather around

dust particles to form clouds. [9]Each droplet of water carries an extremely small amount of electricity. [10]Each ice crystal carries a small amount of electricity also. [11]The clouds gets bigger and heavier. [12]They fill up with electricity. [13]The amount of electricity becomes great enough. [14]The electricity jumps from cloud to cloud. [15]The electricity jumps from a cloud to the Earth. [16]It makes a fantastic spark—LIGHTNING!

Edited paragraph:

_____

_____

_____

_____

_____

_____

_____

_____

_____

_____

_____

_____

_____

_____

_____

PART A *Sharpening Your Word Choices*

Directions: In the paragraph below, more than ten possibilities exist for making changes. Your task is to make at least eight changes. This includes finding four cases where the subject and verb do not agree.

Silver and her group are seldom seen in the place, so how do people know that coyotes lives in the area? One reason are the coyotes' interesting voices that can be heard at night. Silver's sounds often go through the neighborhood until a group of barks, yelps, and howls is returned. Another reason are the occasional discovery of an empty den by interested children. And then there is the occasional missing animals that make the neighbors say, "COYOTE!"

75

(**PART B**) *Editing Your Paragraph*

Sound good?
Combine?
Omit?
Replace?
Expand?

a. As you read the paragraph aloud, ask yourself, "Does it **sound good**?"

b. **Combine** sentences 1 and 2. (Hint: Combine these sentences by using **when** and a **comma**.)

c. Does sentence 3 **sound good**? If not, correct it.

d. **Combine** sentences 4 and 5.

e. Does sentence 7 **sound good**? If not, correct it.

f. **Combine** sentences 7 and 8.

g. **Combine** sentences 11, 12, and 13. (Hint: Combine these sentences by using **or** and by using **but**.)

h. Does sentence 18 **sound good**? If not, correct it.

i. **Combine** sentences 14, 15, 16, 17, 18, and 19. (Hint: Combine these sentences by using **because**, **or**, and **commas**.

¹Follow a few simple rules ²You can feel safe. ³You don't

have to worry about being strucks by lightning. ⁴Remember to

stay away from open spaces. ⁵Don't be the tallest thing around.

⁶Stay away from the water. ⁷So, if you is swimming, get out. ⁸If

you are swimming, go inside. ⁹Don't be near something that

conducts electricity. ¹⁰For example, don't stand under a tree. ¹¹If

you can, go inside a building. ¹²Get into a car. ¹³Stay away from metal. [14]Stay away from telephones and computers. [15]Stay away from televisions. [16]Stay away from appliances. [17]Stay away from bathtubs and showers. [18]Lightning can strike power lines outside and carries electricity into the house. [19]Lightning can strike pipes, too.

Edited paragraph:

_____

_____

_____

_____

_____

_____

_____

_____

_____

_____

_____

_____

_____

_____

Detours

Using the Articles A *and* An

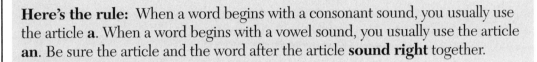

Here's the rule: When a word begins with a consonant sound, you usually use the article **a**. When a word begins with a vowel sound, you usually use the article **an**. Be sure the article and the word after the article **sound right** together.

PART A

1. My friend Josh has a train set.

    My friend Josh has a electric train set.

2. Life is an adjustment for the immigrants.

    Life is an huge adjustment for the immigrants.

3. James is a hardworking employee.

    James is a honest, hardworking employee.

4. The Tigua Indians found nourishment near a river.

    The Tigua Indians found nourishment near a great river.

PART B

CAUTION AHEAD

DETOUR

Directions: After reading each sentence, write **a** or **an** in each blank. Remember to say the article and the word after the article aloud to make sure it sounds right.

1. Glaucoma is _____ disease.

    Glaucoma is _____ eye disease.

2. Cortisone is _____ medication for people with arthritis.

    Cortisone is _____ inexpensive medication for people with arthritis.

3. My grandfather took me on _____ adventure to see new things.

    My grandfather took me on _____ interesting adventure to see new things.

4. After waiting fifteen minutes, we finally stepped into _____ elevator.

    After waiting fifteen minutes, we finally stepped into _____ small elevator.

5. The chorus was preparing for _____ concert.

    The chorus was preparing for _____ upcoming concert.

6. After _____ evening of work, she could hardly wait to get home.

    After _____ hour of evening work, she could hardly wait to get home.

7. My favorite character at Disneyland was _____ pirate with _____ hook for a hand.

    My favorite character at Disneyland was _____ one-eyed pirate with _____ dangerous-looking hook for a hand.

Using a Comma with Coordinate Adjectives

Here's the rule: Use a comma to separate two or more adjectives, **except** when the last adjective is considered part of the noun.

Use this Test: If "and" makes sense between the two adjectives, add a comma.

A.

famous movie star
mysterious twinkling star

B.

small living room
small dark bedroom

C.

yellow school bus
dirty broken-down bus

D. Add a comma or not?

1. courteous store clerk

2. powerful back legs

3. powerful muscular legs

4. steaming hot chocolate

5. hot steaming cocoa

6. white curly-haired sheep

7. loud energetic music

8. loud rock music

9. apricot beaded stole

10. large smooth rock

11. rhythmic rap song

12. soothing harmonious song

13. delicious sweet cream

14. delicious ice cream

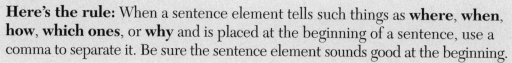

16

Using a Comma to Set Off a Sentence Element at the Beginning of a Sentence

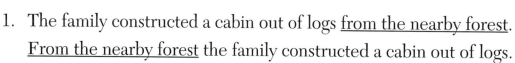

PART A

Here's the rule: When a sentence element tells such things as **where**, **when**, **how**, **which ones**, or **why** and is placed at the beginning of a sentence, use a comma to separate it. Be sure the sentence element sounds good at the beginning.

1. The family constructed a cabin out of logs <u>from the nearby forest</u>.

   <u>From the nearby forest</u> the family constructed a cabin out of logs.

2. Anthropologists examined a shipwreck near North Carolina <u>to find out if Blackbeard really lived</u>.

   <u>To find out if Blackbeard really lived</u> anthropologists examined a shipwreck near North Carolina.

3. Astronaut Michael Collins had to orbit the moon <u>while Neil Armstrong and Buzz Aldrin walked on the moon</u>.

   <u>While Neil Armstrong and Buzz Aldrin walked on the moon</u> astronaut Michael Collins had to orbit the moon.

4. The governor's library was full of history books <u>printed in the 1700s</u>.

   <u>Printed in the 1700s</u> the governor's library was full of history books.

CAUTION
AHEAD

DETOUR

PART B

Directions: Add a comma after each introductory sentence element if it sounds good at the beginning. If it doesn't sound good, cross out the sentence.

1. Even though Roberto Clemente was born in Puerto Rico he played baseball for the Pittsburgh Pirates.

2. When the hurricane finally subsided the entire village was gone.

3. Before Billie Jean King's win over Bobby Riggs no woman had beaten a man in a professional tennis match.

4. Into her locker my sister's backpack lunch and books were crammed.

5. In the Madagascar rain forest 50 species of lemurs leap about.

6. To study cougar behavior biologists placed GPS data transmitters on a number of them.

7. More than 100 years ago the famous San Francisco fire destroyed 28,000 buildings.

8. Because he was exhausted my brother went to bed unusually early.

9. When the spinner dolphins jumped near the boat everyone cheered.

10. Because of global warming engineers are busily searching for cleaner methods of transportation.

26

Using Commas in a Series

Here's the rule: Separate three or more items in a series by adding a comma after each item except the last one.

PART A

1. Jose Jenny and Marcus learned about different breeds of dogs.

2. Dachshunds greyhounds and beagles are hound breeds.

3. Pekingese and toy poodles are types of toy dogs.

4. The children sat quietly listened to the story and laughed.

5. The children stood up and broke into loud applause.

PART B

Directions: Read each sentence. If there are three or more items in a series, add the necessary commas.

1. Megan Joshua and Andrew go to the same school.

2. They have five classes each day: English math social studies science and art.

3. However, they take only English and social studies together.

4. Megan's favorite school activities are reading books painting pictures writing stories and completing science experiments.

5. Joshua enjoys investigating historical events and solving math problems.

6. Each student must have many school supplies including a notebook paper two pencils two pens a yearly calendar a ruler and one art tablet.

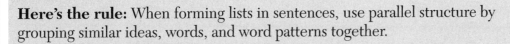

Parallel Structure

PART A

Here's the rule: When forming lists in sentences, use parallel structure by grouping similar ideas, words, and word patterns together.

1. There are many interesting animals in the desert, including <u>kangaroo rats</u>, <u>greater roadrunners</u>, <u>horned lizards</u>, <u>black-tailed jackrabbits</u>, and <u>red rock</u>.

2. There are many interesting animals in the desert, including <u>kangaroo rats</u>, <u>greater roadrunners</u>, <u>horned lizards</u>, <u>black-tailed jackrabbits</u>, and <u>black-tailed deer</u>.

3. Kangaroo rats eat <u>grasses</u> and <u>seed-eating</u>.

4. Kangaroo rats eat <u>grasses</u> and <u>seeds</u>.

5. Kangaroo rats survive the desert because of their abilities <u>to convert</u> dry seeds into water and <u>disposing of</u> waste materials with little output of water.

6. Kangaroo rats survive the desert because of their abilities <u>to convert</u> dry seeds into water and <u>to dispose of</u> waste materials with little output of water.

7. Kangaroo rats have <u>a plump body</u>, <u>large hind legs</u>, and <u>small, rounded ears</u>.

8. Kangaroo rats have <u>a plump body</u>, <u>large hind legs</u>, and <u>hear with small, rounded ears</u>.

36

PART B

CAUTION AHEAD

DETOUR

Directions: Circle the number of the sentence that uses parallel structure.

1. At birth the kangaroo rat is <u>toothless</u>, <u>hairless</u>, and <u>wrinkled</u>.
2. At birth the kangaroo rat is <u>toothless</u>, <u>hairless</u>, and <u>has a lot of wrinkles</u>.

3. When confronted with an enemy, the kangaroo rat might <u>leap into the air</u>, <u>slashing at the enemy with its hind feet</u>, or <u>kick sand at the face of the enemy</u>.
4. When confronted with an enemy, the kangaroo rat might <u>leap into the air</u>, <u>slash at the enemy with its hind feet</u>, or <u>kick sand at the face of the enemy</u>.

5. The roadrunner captures <u>snakes</u>, <u>large insects</u>, <u>rodents</u>, <u>small birds</u>, and <u>chasing lizards that are very fast at running</u>.
6. The roadrunner captures <u>snakes</u>, <u>large insects</u>, <u>rodents</u>, <u>small birds</u>, and <u>fast-running lizards</u>.

7. The roadrunner hunts by <u>walking briskly</u> and <u>running toward its prey</u>.
8. The roadrunner hunts by <u>walking briskly</u> and <u>to run toward its prey</u>.

Parallel Structure

PART A

Here's the rule: When forming lists in sentences, use parallel structure by grouping similar ideas, words, and word patterns together.

1. Observers describe the horned lizard as flat-bodied and looking fierce.

2. Observers describe the horned lizard as flat-bodied and fierce-looking.

3. The horned lizard has a body covered with sharp spines, numerous horns on its head, fringe-like scales along each side of its body, and does not make a good pet.

4. The horned lizard has a body covered with sharp spines, numerous horns on its head, fringe-like scales along each side of its body, and a short tail.

5. Most horned lizards are found in the south-central United States and in northern Mexico.

6. Most horned lizards are found in the south-central United States, and you will find them in northern Mexico.

PART B

Directions: In each sentence, underline the ideas, words, and word patterns that are grouped together. Then, circle the number of the sentence that uses parallel structure.

1. Horned lizards are found in loamy soils or in loose sand.

2. Horned lizards are found in loamy soils or when you look in sand that is loose.

3. Horned lizards dig for three purposes: to hibernate, to build a nest, and to insulate their bodies.

4. Horned lizards dig for three purposes: to hibernate, nesting, and insulation.

5. Jackrabbits like to doze during the hotter part of the day and to forage for food after twilight.

6. Jackrabbits like to doze during the hotter part of the day and foraging for food after twilight.

7. The black-tailed jackrabbit eats cactus, mesquite, and also chomps on grasses.

8. The black-tailed jackrabbit eats cactus, mesquite, and grasses.

9. Their natural enemies include coyotes, foxes, bobcats, badgers, weasels, and they are also eaten by some birds of prey.

10. Their natural enemies include coyotes, foxes, bobcats, badgers, weasels, and large birds of prey.

Using a Comma Before a Coordinating Conjunction

Here's the rule: Add a comma before the conjunctions **but**, **and**, **so**, **or**, **nor**, **for**, or **yet** when the part that comes after could be a stand-alone sentence. (Beware of the **so** with a hidden **that**.)

PART A

1. Since 1999, Nick has won awards for two movies *and* is sure to win more awards.

2. Since 1999, Nick has won awards for two movies *and* he will probably win more awards.

3. My friend Jason is willing to fill his MP3 player with hip-hop and reggae *but* he won't include a single rock-and-roll tune.

4. Mr. Pirelli volunteers forty hours a week at the youth symphony office *so* he can encourage young musicians.

5. Mr. Pirelli volunteers forty hours a week at the youth symphony office *so* he does not have much time at home.

PART B

Directions: Find the conjunction in each sentence and determine whether you need to add a comma. Also, add any other necessary commas.

1. Curling and snowboarding are Winter Olympic sports *but* are not played during the Summer Olympics.

2. When Lucas attended the Summer Olympics in Australia he began the week watching the boxing and wrestling matches *and* he ended the week at the sensational basketball finals.

3. Hot air balloons dirigibles and blimps are called lighter-than-air craft *but* are actually quite heavy.

4. Traveling by hot air balloon is a grand adventure *but* you can't be in a hurry.

5. In the wild adult meerkats bring scorpions to their young *so* they will learn how to capture scorpions for food without being stung.

6. If you were standing on the moon you would see a dark sky *but* you would not see clouds.

7. Chocolate vanilla and strawberry have been the most popular ice cream flavors for many decades *and* are likely to continue as favorites for many years to come.

8. Mr. Ferris created the Ferris wheel in 1892 *so* the United States could have a more fantastic World's Fair than Paris had in 1889.

9. Many people have dogs as pets because dogs are amazingly loyal to their owners *and* can learn complicated entertaining tricks.

10. The Florida Everglades has suffered ecologically for many decades *so* the largest restoration effort in history was launched in the year 2000.

Using Who *or* That

Here's the rule: You usually use **who** to refer to a person or to a specific group of people. You usually use **that** to refer to a thing. Otherwise, choose whichever sounds better.

PART A

1. Businesses **that** hire young workers want employees **who** look responsible.

2. Teenagers **who** wish to be employed often apply at restaurants **that** serve fast food.

3. The teenagers **that** are hired may then join a union **that** campaigns for workers' rights.

4. Employers **who** care about safety will provide training for teens **that** are new to the workplace.

5. Pat, **who** lives down the street, got a job last week at a restaurant **that** opened in her neighborhood.

PART B

Directions: Read each sentence. Write **who** or **that** in each blank.

1. Residents _____ live in dense urban areas often go to parks _____ are maintained by the city or state government.

2. Young children _____ go to these parks particularly enjoy the play equipment _____ allows them a chance to climb.

3. Families _____ go to city parks often bring the equipment _____ is necessary for certain sports.

4. Park visitors _____ are not athletic may bring a book _____ they are currently reading.

5. Some people _____ come to city parks choose to meander on the paths _____ wind through the gardens.

6. Mrs. Jones, _____ visits her neighborhood park daily, loves the gardens _____ always have flowers in bloom.

SENTENCE REFINEMENT CHART

Name _____ Teacher _____

Week _____

First Four Lessons of Each Week (Weeks 1–14)	Part A (5 Participation Points)	Part B (8 Participation Points)	Bonus Points	Total Points (13 possible points)	Lesson Grade
Lesson ___					
Lesson ___					
Lesson ___					
Lesson ___					

Fifth Lesson of Each Week (Weeks 1–14)	Part A (5 Participation Points)	Part B (8 Performance Points)	Bonus Points	Total Points (13 possible points)	Lesson Grade
Lesson ___					
				Weekly Total	Weekly Grade

Participation Points
- Following behavioral guidelines
- Paying attention
- Participating
- Completing work

Performance Points
- no errors .... 8 points
- one error .... 7 points
- two errors .... 6 points
- more than two errors ... 5 points

SENTENCE REFINEMENT CHART

Name _____   Teacher _____

Week _____ *15* _____

All Five Lessons of Week 15	Part A (5 Participation Points)	Part B (8 Performance Points)	Bonus Points	Total Points (13 possible points)	Lesson Grade
Lesson 71					
Lesson 72					
Lesson 73					
Lesson 74					
Lesson 75					
				Weekly Total	Weekly Grade

Total Points for Fifteen Weeks	Overall Grade

Participation Points
- Following behavioral guidelines
- Paying attention
- Participating
- Completing work

Performance Points
- no errors   8 points
- one error   7 points
- two errors   6 points
- more than two errors   5 points